# Germany

# Germany

A documentation

in pictures. Two thousand years of political and cultural development

by Götz Fehr and Werner Rehfeld          Bruckmann München

In Cooperation with Inter Nationes e. V. Bonn, Bad Godesberg
© Copyright 1970 publishing house F. Bruckmann KG, Munich
All rights reserved, including translation,
photomechanical reproduction, including extracts
Overall Production: F. Bruckmann KG, Printing works for graphic art, Munich
Paper Feldmühle AG
Serial No: ISBN 3 7654 1297 x Printed in Germany

Germany consists of a floor of Paleozoic rocks upon which rest uncomfortably the comparatively little-disturbed beds of the Mesozoic system, while in the north German plain a covering of glacial deposits conceals the whole of the older strata from view, excepting some scattered and isolated outcrops of Cretaceous and Tertiary beds.

Encyclopaedia Britannica

The Germans love and respect nature. They tend towards melancholy and sadness.

From an opinion-poll in France

The Germans enthuse about nature, only because there are so many pubs there.

Henry F. Urban   USA

Germany is a very masculine country. Within a few days of arrival one quickly realises that the Germans describe their homeland in song, poetry and in the vernacular as fatherland, not, like many other nations, motherland.

Pura Santillan Castrence   Philippines

Germany is the India of the Western World.

Victor Hugo   France

The tension between Germany and France, the most persistent on the continent, is the main distinguishing feature of Europe's psychological landscape...
This contrast between prevailing tendencies in the way of thinking of the Germans and French condemns them to a permanent tension which is dangerous but also fruitful. Their feeling for fluctuation leads the Germans

into constant change, their feeling for form causes the French to reject this change. The Germans remain permanently in touch with the sources and origins of their fluctuating lives. The French, on the other hand, appear always to have reached the end of life, where there is nothing more to say, to wish for, to think about and above all to change.

Salvador de Madariaga   Spain

Apart from their diligence, ability and orderliness, there is a further characteristic which endears the Germans to the Swedes. It is what the Germans call their "heartfelt ties with nature." Both the Swedes and the Germans are nature romanticists of the first order. If there is any difference at all, then it is merely the German tendency to make an almost indigestible programme out of their inborn love of nature.

Agne Hamrin   Sweden

Cooperation with Germany: nothing would be more desirable for both countries than that each should possess what the other lacks.

André Gide   France

The German—that is for me another word for work. It is sufficient to cast an eye over the cities which, we know, were almost completely destroyed and which are today flourishing communities. There is something miraculous about this: Germany has worked.

Flavien Ranaivo   Madagascar

The last 25 years have radically altered the heterogenous and manifold nature of the German people. The inner migration happened in greater measure than elsewhere. The war, the expulsion of thirteen million Germans from the original eastern territories and Sudetenland, and finally from the Soviet Zone to West Germany, have almost completely obliterated the former tribal boundaries. The technical age is about to make "Germans" out of the people of Bavaria, Swabia, Franconia, Hesse, Rhineland and Lower Saxony.

Peter Dürrenmatt   Switzerland

National economists will be studying the causes of the German "economic miracle" for a long time to come; the surprising effect of the currency reform, the influence of American Marshall Aid, the purposeful organisation and intelligent reconstruction of industry. But they should not forget the inner discipline of the ordinary German or his readiness, without grumbling, to fulfil difficult tasks, even when he cannot hope for high wages.

Albert Joh. Marie van Dal   Netherlands

The German has a definite feeling of belonging to the whole, gains satisfaction and fulfils his ambition from the fact that he is an undoubtedly small but, in his way, an irreplaceable cog in a precisely functioning machine. German diligence and zeal in their work had successfully passed the test immediately after the war: at that time poverty, hopelessness and wretchedness prevailed. People paid with worthless money, the future was, to say the least, uncertain, but the Germans did not allow themselves to be eaten up, in the core of their character, by the general demoralization of defeat. They continued working in their own way, and this has taken them once more to the top... Stefan Kisielewski   Poland

As ever, the German way of life is distinguished by a precisely planned alternation of concentration and relaxation. But whereas nowadays they appear to relax at work, they concentrate the whole of their talent for organization of their free-time.

Arthur Miller   USA

Everyone in Italy knows, of course, about the Germany of the economic miracle, but one is tempted to look behind this superficial image of prosperity and economic growth for a Germany, conservative by preference but not particularly reactionary. Few people are aware of the fact that Germany, today, is one of the most socially progressive countries in the West.

Pietro Quaroni   Italy


There are hopeful signs which point to the fact that the Germans will soon no longer be diligent and efficient, but will become as idle and carefree as we English.

Malcolm Muggeridge   Great Britain


The Germans are unhappy when things are going well.

André François-Poncet   France


I have often experienced employees taking unfinished work home – I cannot rid myself of the impression that they feel lost and bored without such work in their leisure time. There are sufficient institutions in Germany which teach how to work – but where are the Germans to learn how to organise and enjoy their free-time?

Prodosh Aich   India


Nothing is taken more seriously in Germany than the preparations for fun.

Henri Blondeau   France


Germany takes everything to extremes. She distinguishes herself through a lack of equilibrium both in bad and good.   Romain Rolland   France


Occupying one's time fully is the merit of the Germans, forgetting it is the talent of the French.

Germaine de Staël   France


One day my daughter was dancing with a German. When she said something he did not understand, he stopped in the middle of the dance-floor, took out his dictionary and looked it up.   From an opinion-poll in Italy


The German is by no means sober-minded and efficient, governed solely by his reason. He is also a man of action whereby the forces of his mind and the depths of his feeling impart impulses to his organisational and creative achievements.

Peter Dürrenmatt   Switzerland


The Germans are honest and open, they speak their mind clearly. But since they are, or want to be too thoroughly honest, they take no heed of whether it could destroy the harmony of society or whether their forthrightness could be unpleasant and embarrassing to others; the Germans are poor at flattery and paying compliments.
And a further quality of the Germans which strikes the Japanese; they would like questions wherever possible to be clearly decided with yes or no, good or bad, right or wrong. To leave something unclear or just to wait until nature or time solves the matter – this is something the Germans cannot do. They pronounce their opinions, theories or doctrines until they end up in a cul-de-sac.

Kazuo Kani   Japan


The gift of emotional involvement: that is the possibility for Germans to answer the call of reality, to join in the music, to swing in the waves of others, of the intimate. The Germans have proved, in good measure, this talent for emotional involvement in all fields of art and science by their creative achievements… And in reality, throughout their whole history, the Germans have foreseen the future by viewing the present and have known how to extract from this new thoughts and forms of the future.

Here lies the significance of their contribution to European culture yesterday and to that of the world tomorrow.

Léopold Sédar Senghor   Senegal

The expression in the German's heart has remained coarse and violent.

George Santayana   USA

The Germany I love and which has fertilized my intellect is the Germany of great world citizens.

Romain Rolland   France

I am of the opinion that the Germans possess an honesty of intellect which places their science above all others.

Ralph Waldo Emerson   USA

What is it about present-day Germany that attracts me? Eternal Germany? Well, I believe it is her cultured essence, her open-minded attitude, her progress in science and technology and the simultaneous preservation of her devotion to music, her intuitive grasp and her poetic potential, her love of good cooking, of good wine and good beer and finally her regional variety within her basic unity. From this point of view, Germany is a nation for whom the Iberio-Romans, to which I belong with heart and soul, experience a deeper and wider affinity, which goes far beyond the purely intellectual, than for the Scandinavians, Dutch, Belgians and even the English and the French.

Gilberto Freyre   Brazil

The southerner who comes to Germany calms down and soothes his nerves in an eternal bath of peace, in the gentleness of blonde colours and the tranquility of movement which characterizes the Germans, in their orderliness and regularity, which is likewise therapeutic. Points and sharp edges do not exist here. But the most salutary effect on the southerner is the impression imparted by this people, on the streets and in their gardens, that they exist because of each other. What really lives in the streets and gardens is society.

Zacharias Papantoniu   Greece

Following the capitulation, the Federal Republic of Germany established a dynamic, free economy and a bulwark of freedom on the ruins of tyranny.

John F. Kennedy   USA

The Germany of today is not the Germany of yesterday.

David Ben Gurion   Israel

In my view a German community is developing in which public opinion is playing, in increasing measure, an important role – a public opinion backed by a better balance between ambition and nonchalance, a balance, too, between the diverse forces in society which have learnt now to get along together.

Terence Prittie   Great Britain

What attracts the Greek to the German is not the feeling of an identical view of life or a related way of life but rather an instinct emanating from him for the fruitfulness of tension. He is drawn to the English by their sporting attitude to life, the love of the game and competition, the contempt for work and the quality of positive laziness. Latins fascinate him by the mutuality of mistakes and vice. The German, on the other hand, remains quite simply "the other person," whose hard manner of speech, discipline and objectivity, which the Greeks often find cold, make contact so difficult. Where is the German's heart? The Greek does not always find this question easy to answer and this irritates him. Since, however, he is open to the ambivalence of life's values, he does not exclude himself from the positive side of these qualities. For it is in this very German that his unhappy love of orderliness encounters supplementary qualities which he needs for self-enhancement.

Johannes Gaitanides   Greece

The German loves to issue instructions to his fellow-citizens; he likes to display his superiority and plays the schoolmaster. If, however, he meets opposition with a better argument he gives way quickly and sensibly. This is not just a sign of intelligence but of intellectual honesty.

Pura Santillan Castrence   Philippines

German society seems, for the most part, to have freed itself from its patriarchal stamp. The German is now less humble to his superiors, has gained in self-confidence.        Albert Joh. Marie van Dal   Netherlands

In a post-war period, characterized otherwise by extreme political upheavals, the Germans have succeeded in giving themselves an internal and external constitution on the road to true democracy. The attainment of their own freedom is the greatest success ever achieved by the German people – it has at last discovered itself.

Horacio G. Lebrón   Paraguay

Following their experiences of national socialist tyranny, the Germans have a panic-stricken fear of state intervention in the economy, journalism and private life.

Bohumil Cerny   Czechoslovakia

It was not their acquaintance with the material side of life which made the strongest impression on the four Soviet journalists... They were much more impressed by the natural efforts of every ordinary person in West Germany to live in peace and on friendly terms with other races.        Alexei Adjubey   USSR

The Germans are a great and courageous people. Their diligence, their science and bravery demand the admiration of the world. We hope that they will lead a movement for peace. They were beaten in the last war, but not conquered. Their legendary energy must only be guided into the right channels so that they can promote the progress of the world as a whole.

Mahatma Gandhi   India

Truly, you Germans have done enough for the history of the world.        Winston Churchill   Great Britain

As a divided nation, the Germans have to overcome a greater task than other Europeans. They are already in the middle of this task, whilst their new state has, by no means, been consolidated and overcoming twelve years of national socialism, essential for a clear relationship to history, is still in its infancy. The German people must learn to believe in themselves and their unity, without falling prey to a revival of ardent nationalism, and then progressing with compromises on a short-term basis, day by day. At one and the same time, they must display their ability to master their situation between Latin and Slavic Europe by federal means and without resorting to force. A formidable task! It demands the rebirth of a strong feeling for life. It must come from the intellect, from the European basic question: How do we keep abreast of the times? That is the question of the age.

Peter Dürrenmatt   Switzerland

I congratulate you on being young Germans, children of a great nation. Yes, a great nation that has made great mistakes in the course of its history. A nation, however, that has presented the world with rewarding intellectual, scientific, artistic and philosophic waves and enriched it with the countless products of its powers of invention, its technology and its work; a nation that in its peaceful activity as well as in the sufferings of war, has unfolded a true wealth of courage, discipline and organisation.

Charles de Gaulle   France

A new generation is growing up in Germany, which is not prepared to accept special restrictions. Sooner or later young Germans will turn against inequality and discrimination; then no nation as proud and capable as the German wants to be indefatigable hostages of history and we would indeed be foolish if we considered anything else possible.   George Wildman Ball   USA

The Germans, even the most likeable, may appear contradictory and difficult to understand to foreigners trapped in the undergrowth of prejudices. On the other hand it is easier to get to know and very much easier to grow to love their country and what they have made of it.

Christine M. Totten   USA

A European federation of states, a hundred times, yes! An atomized Germany in a non-united Europe – danger and nonsense!   Victor Gollanz   Great Britain

**Structures**         **Land of Encounter**

Explanatory notes on the illustrations are to be found on pages 319-332

Germany, lying in the heart of Europe

Land between the alps in the south

Intersected by huge rivers,

5  *The Danube near*
   *Werenwag Castle*

6  *The Elbe near*
   *Blankenese*

9　*Palatinate forest and Trifels Castle*

7　*A beechwood forest in the Spessart*

8　*Southern part of the Black Forest*

10   *Lüneburg Heath*

11   *A volcanic lake in the Eifel mountains*   25

*12  A valley near Höfats
in the Allgäu*

26

shaped

13  *Nördlingen
    in the Ries basin*

by man

14 *Duisburg*

28

# Settled since olden times

*16  Franconian ornamental disc*     *17  Lake-dwellings at Unteruhldingen on Lake Constance*

18 *Cairns on the Lüneburg Heath*

19 *Foundations of a Roman villa*

# Homeland of different tribes

20 *Traditional dress in Mühlenbach*

21 *Black Forest farmhouse*

22 *Farmhouse in Eiderstedt, Friesland*       23 *Traditional dress in Lindhorst, near Bückeburg*

24 *Fields near Lörrach*

25  *Industrial installations in Rheinhausen*    *overleaf: 26  Bayer Works at Leverkusen*

27 *Frontier check-point on the German-Belgian autobahn near Aachen*

*28  Border between the Federal Republic of Germany and the German Democratic Republic near Lauenstein*   39

29  *Lake Constance*

*30  Bridge over the Fehmarn Sound*  41

# Land of Encounter

Germany's variety is the result
of the mixture and overlapping
of different tribes and cultures

31  *Celtic sand pillar from Pfalzfeld*    32  *Runic stone from Haithabu*    33  *Franconian gravestone from Niederdollendorf*

35 *The Basilica in Trier*

34 *Lothar's cross with Augustinian cameo*

# Byzantium

36  *Otto II receiving homage from the provinces*    37  *Royal hall in Lorsch monastery*

all exercised their influence as did the missionary work of Irish monks

38  *Portal of the Scottish church of St. Jacob in Regensburg*          39  *Evangelist symbols*

Even in the 4<sup>th</sup> century there were

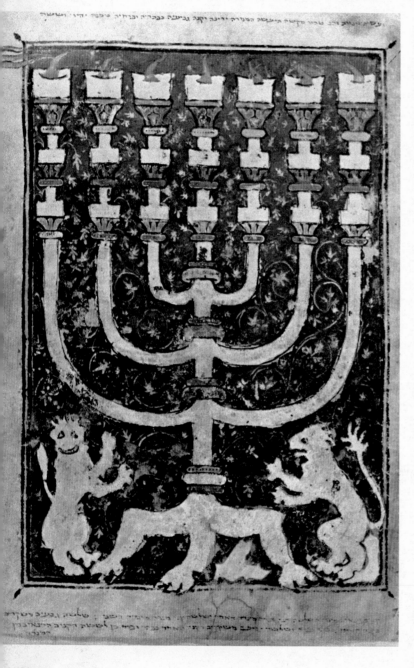

*40 Seven-branched candlestick from a Hebrew manuscript*

*Jnpator redit dans Judeis legē moysi i rotulo.*

42 *Henry VII presenting the Jews with the Mosaic Law*

41 *Mikwe in Friedberg, Hesse*

43 *Ceiling of the hall of prayer in Horb*

# At all times Germany played an important role as mediator

44 *Roland slaying a heathen*

45 *Konrad von Altstätten*

46 *Cologne Cathedral, West façade*

47  *Archbishop Peter of Aspelt crowning John of Luxembourg,*
    *King of Bohemia*

48  *Saint Elizabeth helping the poor*

49  *Head of a Bohemian Madonna*

50  *The »Landshut Wedding«*

52  *Douvermann: St. Mary Magdalene*

53  *Heidelberg Castle,*
*Ottheinrichs-Wing*

54 *Nordic
half-timbered houses:
street in
Soden-Allendorf*

55 *Mediterranean
stone architecture
houses in Wasserbu
on the Inn*

54

# Italian baroque found its German expression

*56  West façade of Passau Cathedral*

57 *Music room, Sanssouci Palace*

58 *The gardens of Nymphenburg Castle*

*»In my state everyone can be happy in his own way«.*

# As the country with the most neighbours in the world

above: *63  José Ortega y Gasset   64  Benedetto Croce   65  Max Born*   below: *66  Henry van de Velde   67  Igor Stravinsky   68  J. Robert Oppenheimer*

# Germany became a second homeland for many people of other races

above: *69 Florence Nightingale 70 Feodor Dostoyevsky 71 Lenin* below: *72 Edvard Munch 73 Lyonel Feininger 74 Olaf Gulbransson* 61

# Also nowadays as a land of encounter

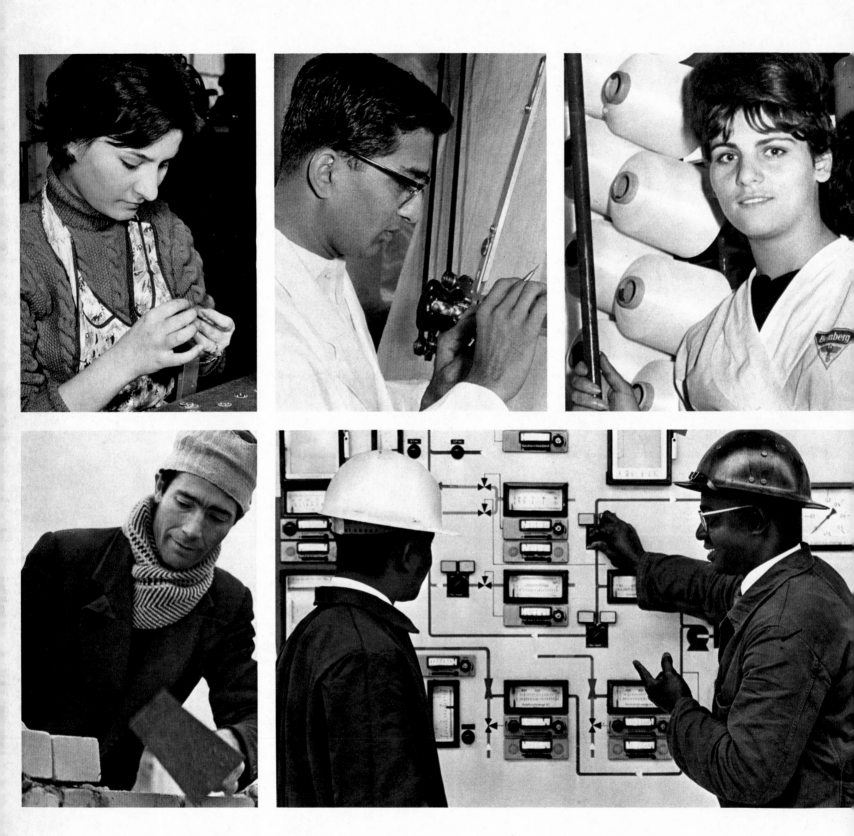

75–79   *Trainees, foreign workers*

# Society yesterday and today

# The peasants

82  *Vergil of Strasbourg,*
*Peasants Ploughing*

83  *Albrecht Dürer, Wire Mill*

84  *Half-timbered houses in Freudenberg, Hesse*  67

# Although oppressed by feudal lords, the peasants succeeded

85  Rebel peasants
taking a knight prisoner

87  Monument commemorating
the victory of
the Dithmarschen peasants

86  The »Free Imperial Village« of Gochsheim          88  Court of freemen near Kaichen, Hesse

# Peasant customs and art reflect the variety of the German tribes

91  *Bed from Lake Schlier*

93  *Graffiti in Oberhörl*

92  *Headboards in Arnbruck*

94  *Westerwald dish*

95 *Lime blossom festival
in Schenklengsfeld*

96 *Hopfield*    97 *Vineyards on the slopes of the Tuniberg*    98 *Cornfield*

99  *New structures
   in an old landscape,
   Allgäu*

# The Church

Monastic orders in the early Middle Ages pioneered the development of a systematic agricultural economy. They removed from work in the fields the stigma of being the fate of slaves

100  *Jörg Breu, St. Bernhard and monks working in the fields*

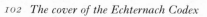

*102  The cover of the Echternach Codex*

*103  The initial L from the Munich Codex Clm 4433*

AETHERNA IPSE SVAE MENTIS SIMVLACHRA LVTHERVS
EXPRIMIT·AT VVLTVS CERA LVCAE OCCIDVOS
·M·D·X·X·

104  *Henricus de Alemannia teaching at the Sorbonne*     105  *Martin Luther*

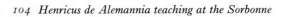

106  *Chair of Albertus Magnus, Regensburg*

82     *107  Stucco angel in the church of Zwiefalten on the Danube*

# The protestant parsonage

109  *Gotthold Ephraim Lessing*

110  *Friedrich Hölderlin*

111  *Georg Friedrich Wilhelm Hegel*

112  *Theological Seminary of Tübingen*

113  Friedrich Wilhelm
     Josef von Schelling

114  Friedrich Nietzsche

115  Gottfried Benn

116  Main church in Wolfenbüttel

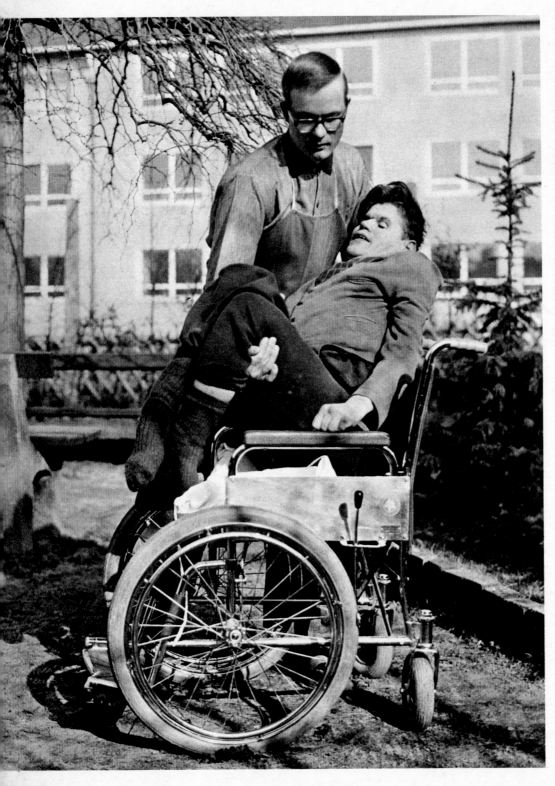

*118  Friedrich von Bodelschwingh*

*117  Bethel near Bielefeld*

# Education in the spirit of responsibility

120   *Nikolaus, Count of Zinzendorf*

121   *Herrnhut Community*

122   *Protestant Academy, Bad Boll*

*124  Deed of Charlemagne*

90          *125  Knights jousting*

of the Franconian army and the feudal system, the aristocracy determined

26  *Ekkehard and Uta*
    *in Naumburg*
    *Cathedral*

127 *Eltz Castle*

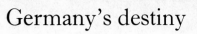

# for a thousand years

128 *Landgrave's choir in the Elizabeth Church, Marburg*

129 *Moated castle in Gemen, Westphalia*

# The State of the Teutonic Knights

Chivalry
and christian
missionary work
led the Order
of Teutonic Knights
to found a
monastic State
in East Prussia

130  *The great refectory of*
     *the Teutonic Knights in*
     *Marienburg Castle*

# The elective kingdom

*131 Relief of electors*

True to old traditions, the German kings were elected by representatives of the aristocracy

*132 The royal rostrum in Rhens on the Rhine*

*133  Elector Frederick the Wise, Martin Luther and Ulrich Zwingli*

135 *Christian of Brunswick-Wolfenbüttel*
*with the cities conquered by him*

*136
Staircase
in Brühl
Castle near
Cologne*

140  *Wall pavilion of the Zwinger, Dresden*

# Members of the aristocracy

142 Karl, Imperial Baron
vom und zum Stein

143 Wilhelm Emanuel, Baron von Ketteler

144 Claus, Count Schenk
von Stauffenberg

141 Heinrich, Baron von Gagern

*145 Thurn and Taxis postage stamps*

*146 Thurn and Taxis carriage museum in Regensburg* 103

# The citizens

German town-life in the early Middle Ages began
in the former Roman cities on the Rhine and
Danube where the consciousness of the civil
liberties of the Civis Romanus had never been eradicated.

147 *The Porta Nigra in Trier*

## Diß sind der Statt
Cöllen alte Recht vnd Burger Frey-
heiten/ als hernach beschrieben volgen.

### Die Statt Cölln ist ein freye Reichs-
statt/ vnd ihre Burger freye Königliche Burger.

Rstlich ist zuwissen / daß ein
Statt von Cöllen ein freye Reichs-
Statt/ vñ alle Burger freye Königliche
Burger sein/ vnd frey gehuld / von einem Römischen König/ also daß man
kein Burger/Burgersche oder Jngeses-
sen in Cöllen mit gewalt vber Recht be-
schweren soll,

### Burger vnuerhört nicht zufangen
noch zu Thurnen.

Vm andern ist der Statt Recht vnd Burger Freyheit/
daß ein Raht zur zeit keinen Burger straffen/ fangen/
angreiffen/ noch zu Thurn führen soll/ vmb keiner sa-
chen willen/ deren er vbersagt mag werden/ was auch das
were/ der Raht soll dann ersten den Burger besenden/ vnd
lassen ihm die vbersagung fürlegen/ vnd kund thun/ vnd ver-
hören sein antwort/ vnd wann er sich dann nicht wolt ver-
antworten/ so soll man ihm gebieten vnd sagen/ daß er mit
der Sonnen auff einen der Statt Thurn gehe/ vnd lassen
ihn

148 *Civil liberties of the city of Cologne*

# As communities of free burghers,

150   *Statue of Roland in front of Bremen town hall*

151   *Eagle on the market fountain, Goslar*

152   *Figures of sentinels above the town hall entrance in Regensburg*

157
City wall
of Rothenburg
ob der Tauber

158
Patricians'
houses
in Lübeck

159
*Self-portrait:*
*Adam Krafft*

160 *The "Nuremberg Egg"*    161 *The public weigher: relief by Adam Krafft*    162 *Bakers' Guild tankard*    163 *Guild panel of the Master Dyers*     113

Social institutions still in existence today

# The town hall remained throughout the centuries

168 Cologne
council meeting
at the beginning
of the 17th century

170 Town hall square
in Lübeck

169 Council meeting
in Ulm

Industrialisation threatened the craftsman in his existence.
The social plight of this class became known all over
Germany by the uprising of the Silesian weavers.

*179  Käthe Kollwitz: The protest march of the Silesian weavers*

180   Otto Dix: My father – my mother

# against degrading working conditions

*181  Mechanical forge near Wegscheid*   *182  Works shop-floor about 1910*

# Karl Marx and Friedrich Engels embodied the demands of the underprivileged in a political programme

*185 Birthplace of Karl Marx in Trier*     *186 Title page of the first edition of the "Manifesto of the Communist Party"*

# Likewise members of the churches and provincial parliaments strove for reforms

187  *Adolf Kolping*

188  *Johann Hinrich Wichern*

189  *Friedrich Engels*

190  *Franz Joseph von Buß*

191 *May Day poster of 1901*

130    192 *May Day Celebrations 1966 in Berlin*

193  *Centenary Celebrations of the Trade Unions*

*194  Leaflet commemorating the Congress of Unification of the German Social Democrats in Gotha, 1875*

*195  Statute of the German Workers' Union*        *196  Kurt Schumacher*

197  *Cooperative society store in Chemnitz*

198  *Student hostel of the Workers'*
*Welfare Organisation*

# The stage awakened the social conscience of the nation

**Verein Freie Bühne.**

Sonntag, den 26. Februar 1893
Mittags 12 Uhr
im
Neuen Theater.

## Die Weber.

Schauspiel aus den vierziger Jahren in fünf Aufzügen von
Gerhart Hauptmann.

| | |
|---|---|
| Dreißiger, Parchend-Fabrikant | Hr. Nissen. |
| Frau Dreißiger | Frl. Kötschau. |
| Weinhold, Hauslehrer | Hr. Eisfeld. |
| Pfeifer, Expedient | Hr. Fischer. |
| Neumann, Cassirer | Hr. Helgen. |
| Der Lehrling | Hr. Haller. |
| Der Kutscher | Hr. Liebnitz. |
| Ein Mädchen | Frl. Wertheim. |
| Pastor Kittelhaus | Hr. Pagay. |
| Frau Pastor Kittelhaus | Fr. Berg. |
| Heide, Polizeiverwalter | Hr. Beaurepaire. |
| Kutsche, Gensdarm | Hr. Hagemann. |
| Welzel, Gastwirth | Hr. Hummel. |
| Frau Welzel | Frau Berg. |
| Anna Welzel | Frau Hachmann-Zipser. |
| Wiegand, Tischler | Hr. Waldemar. |
| Ein Reisender | Hr. Worlitzsch. |
| Ein Bauer | Hr. C. Pauli. |
| Ein Förster | Hr. Burgard. |
| Schmidt, Chirurgus | Hr. Tielscher. |
| Hornig, Lumpensammler | Hr. Theodor Müller. |
| Der alte Wittig, Schmiedemeister | Hr. Pauly. |
| Bäcker | Hr. Vorwerk. |
| Moritz Jäger | Hr. Rittner. |
| Der alte Baumert | Hr. H. Pauli. |
| Mutter Baumert | Fr. Brehm. |
| Bertha Baumert | Frl. Pauli I. |
| Emma Baumert | Frl. Pauli II. |
| Fritz, Emma's Sohn, (4 Jahre alt) | Gretchen Müller. |
| August Baumert | Hr. Hermes. |
| Der alte Ansorge | Hr. Löwenfeld. |
| Frau Heinrich | Frl. Reichenbach. |
| Der alte Hilse | Hr. Höck. |
| Frau Hilse | Fr. Becker-Nelidoff. |
| Gottlieb Hilse | Hr. Hellmuth-Braem. |
| Luise, Gottlieb's Frau | Frl. Bertens. |
| Mielchen, Tochter, (6 Jahre alt) | Trudchen Müller. |
| Reimann, Weber | Hr. Ludwig. |
| Heiber, Weber | Hr. Stollberg. |
| Eine Weberfrau | Fr. Werner. |
| | Hr. Gaspart. |
| | Hr. Paulmüller. |
| Weber | Hr. Seldenek. |
| | Hr. Reichenbach. |
| | Hr. Nauendorf. |
| | Hr. Haid. |
| Ein Knabe | Kl. Pauli. |
| Junge Weberfrauen | Frl. Delbrück. |
| | Frl. Reiner. |
| | Frl. Zimmermann. |

Weber und Weberfrauen.

Die Vorgänge dieser Dichtung geschehen in den vierziger Jahren in Kaschbach im Eulen-
gebirge, sowie in Peterswaldau und Langenbielau am Fuße des Eulengebirges.

Regie: Cord Hachmann.

Die große Pause findet nach dem dritten Akte statt.

*199 Programme of the premiere of "The Weavers" in 1893*     *200 Bert Brecht, "Puntila and his servant Matti"*

201　*Max von der Grün, "State of emergency, or the strolling players are coming"*

# Master, not slave of the technical world?

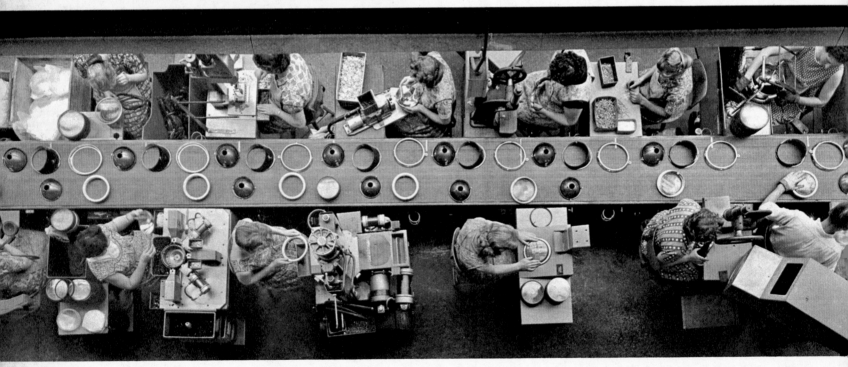

# Society in a changing world

Two world wars, inflation, a currency reform, the destruction of the cities and the expulsion of millions of Germans from Eastern Europe have fundamentally changed society. In the modern industrial society, in addition to workers, salaried classes and civil servants, it is predominantly members of the intellectual professions who determine public life.

*206 Bank note of the time of the inflation* *207 Refugees, 1945* *208 Buried under rubble* *209 "Hohe Straße" in Cologne*

The idea of the Empire —— The empire of ideas

# The Holy Roman Empire of the German Nation

From the tradition of the Roman Empire, the first
emperors took over the task of preserving peace and
justice and the propagation of Christianity.
The joint rule of Pope and Emperor within
the Holy Roman Empire of the German Nation
safeguarded order in the Western world.

211  *Charlemagne*

212  *The Pope and the Emperor on a joint throne*

213  *Charlemagne's throne in Aachen Cathedral*

144

214  *The Lepanto Monstrance*

215  *St. Ulrich's Cross*

216  *Turkish war booty of the Margrave Ludwig Wilhelm von Baden*

## The »Imperial Court Errant« demanded the establishment of Free Imperial cities

In the cause of the supra-national conception of the empire,
the emperors were permanently on the move.
Although the empire had no fixed capital,
many imperial palaces subsequently became
the germ-cells of the Free Imperial cities, whose citizens
were subject to the emperor alone.

*217   Group of windows in the main hall of the Imperial Castle at Wimpfen*

*218   The Emperor's living room in Nuremburg Castle*

219 *The Imperial*
*Cathedral*
*in Worms,*
*East Choir*

149

# The Empire collapsed when it assumed the dimensions of a world power

The empire of Emperor Charles V extended from Hungary to America. The growing power of the German princes and the religious disputes led to the breaking up of the unity of the Habsburg Empire within Germany. The Thirty Years' War led finally to Germany's political disintegration.

220   *Titian, Emperor Charles V*

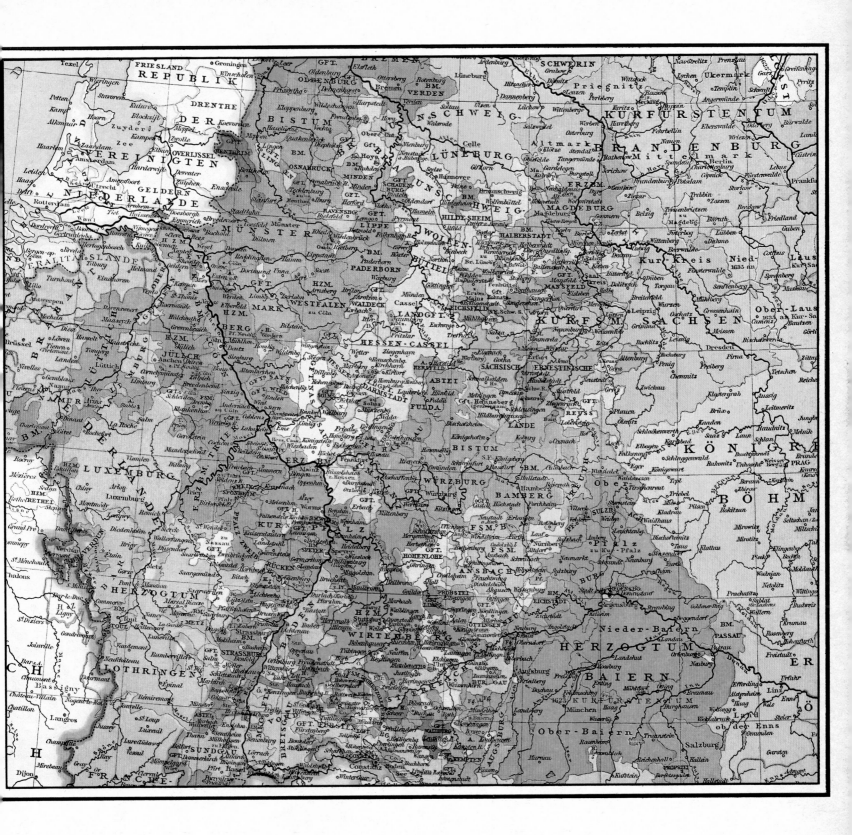

*222  The Hall of the Imperial Diet in the town hall, Regensburg*

*223  Empress Maria Theresia*
*224  Frederick II, the Great*    *225  The Imperial court room in Würzburg*

Whereas the old idea of the Empire led to the creation of an Austrian State, embracing several nations,

Prussia developed into a new centre of political order in Germany

The state attitude, based on public welfare and tolerance in Prussia, made diligence, fulfilment of duty, honesty

and obedience the essence of one's way of life, represented above all by the civil servants.    *226  Charlottenburg Palace, Berlin*

227  *Andreas Schlüter, statue of the Elector Frederick William*     228  *Crown Princess Louisa of Prussia*     229  *"Prince Frederick of Homburg"*     155

# The renewal of the Empire as a liberal, national state

The struggle against Napoleon aroused patriotism and civic consciousness. In 1848 revolution broke out all over Germany followed subsequently by the establishment of a parliament in Frankfurt. The Prussian king's refusal to accept the imperial crown from the hands of representatives

*230  Statue commemorating the Battle of Leipzig (1813)*     *231  Barricade-fighting in the revolution of 1848*

# was defeated by the opposition of the German Princes

of the people, denied the revolution its success. Following Austria's defeat, in 1866, Prussia became the leading power in Germany. Count Bismarck's policy lead, in 1871, to the Prussian king being proclaimed German Emperor.

232  *Count Otto von Bismarck*      233  *The National Assembly in St. Paul's Church, Frankfurt-on-Main, 1848*      157

# The age of Nationalism perverted

Bismarck's idea of an empire in the form of a national state mediating between east and west was not realised. The feudal structure of the two German empires proved unable to withstand the challenge and burden of World War I. Following their defeat in 1918, Germany and Austria became republics.
The Treaty of Versailles, hitherto unsuspected economic difficulties and the growth of political radicalism drove Germany into destruction at the hands of National Socialist tyranny.

*234  Statue of Hermann in Detmold, Westphalia*

# the idea of the Empire

237  Josef Thorak's studio

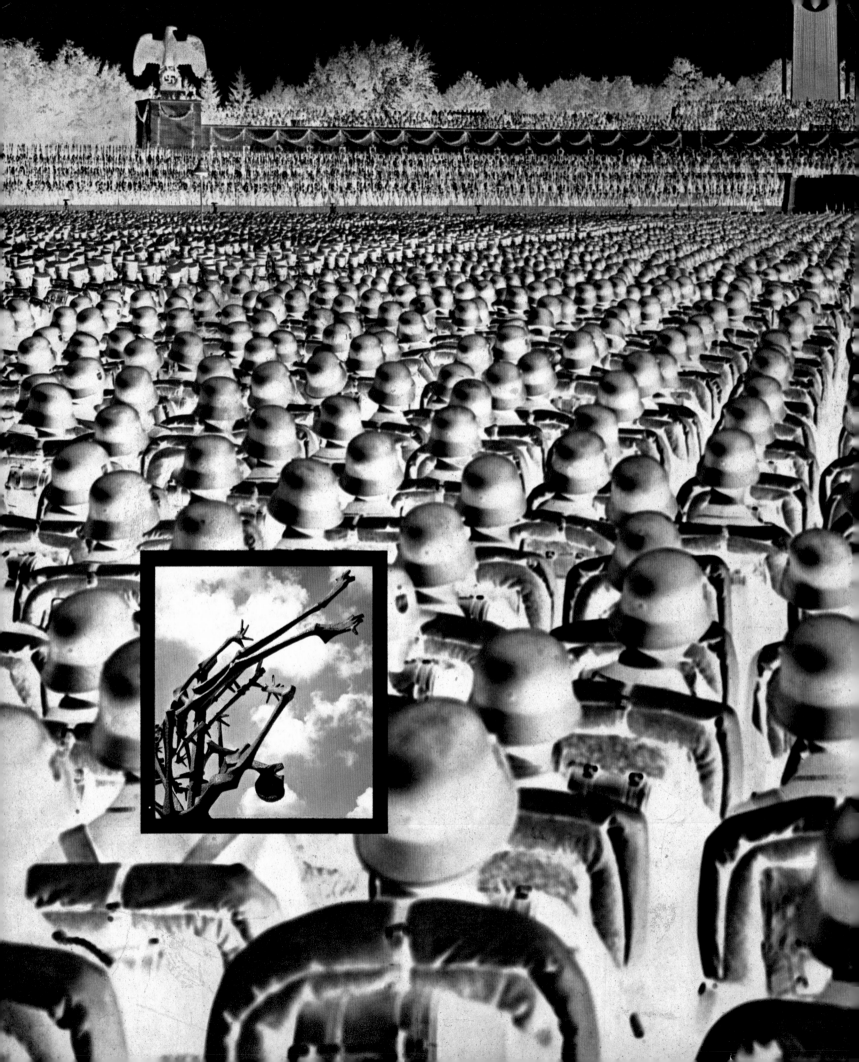

# Out of the catastrophe of World War II, out of the rubble of Europe

242 *Corpus Christi procession in Cologne, 1946*

grew a realistic concept of a European community

244  *Meeting of the Council of Europe in Strasbourg*

245 *Robert Schumann, Alcide de Casperi and Konrad Adenauer*

246 *Paul-Henri Spaak*   247 *Walter Hallstein*   243 *The Trans-Europa Express*

# The association of ideas:

## Gemeener
## Borger-Eed,
### der
## Stadt Bremen.

Ick will dem Rahde gehorsam syn und num-
mermehr jegen den Rahd dohn, ock in allen Nöhden
und Gefahr, so düsser goden Stadt nu und in künff-
tig, vorstahn und begegnen mögen, dem Rahde, ock
gemeener Stadt und Borgerschup, trouw und holdt
syn; Ick will ock tho nenem Uprohr Ohrsake geven, noch my
dartho versellschoppen; Sondern wohr ick Uprohr, oder sonst
enige Practiken offte heimlike Anschläge, jegen düsse gode Stadt
erfahre, will Ick dem Rahde trouwliken vermelden, und holden
Taffeln und Boeck, mit der Nyen upgerichteden Eendracht, alse
de de Rahd und gantze Meenheit beschwaren hebben; Ick will
recht ziesen und schatten, ock recht consumeren, so lange solke
Consumption, mit Belevung Eenes Ehrenvesten Rahds und der
Borgerschup, im Gebruke blifft; Minem Hövetmanne und
Rottmeister, ock anderen des Rahdes Befehlhebbern, geböhr-
liken Gehorsam leisten; Und will also des Rahdes, und gemeener
Stadt Beste wehten und befordern, dargegen öhren Schaden und
Rahdehl wehren und affkehren, nah allem mynen Vermögen.
Dit Gewehr, darmede Ick vor Enem Ehrenvesten Rahde erschiene,
dat is mien eegen, datsülve will Ick nicht verringern, sondern
bestes mines Vermögens verbetern: So wahr helpe my GOtt!

*248 "Communal Citizens' Oath of the City of Bremen"*

# Unity . . .

249 *Taking the civic oath*

251 *The Hambach Festival, 1832*

252 *Ferdinand Hodler, "Vow of unity"*

254  *The market cross in Trier*

253  *Medieval court of justice in the town hall, Lüneburg*

255 *Swearing-in Theodor Heuss*     256 *A scen e from the Code of Old Saxon Laws*

257 *Chair of the high court of justice, Rottweil*

and freedom,

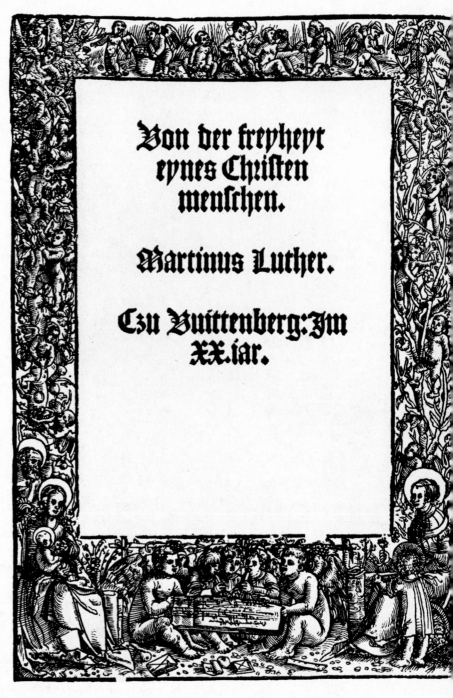

260 *Title page of the first impression of Martin Luther's*
*pamphlet entitled "Concerning the Freedom of a Christian"*

258 *Freedom banner of the Peasants' Revolt*     259 *Civil liberties on the doors of Mainz Cathedral*

## Der heſſiſche Landbote.

### Erſte Botſchaft.

Darmſtadt, im Nov. 1834.

**Friede den Hütten! Krieg den Paläſten!**

Im Jahr 1834 ſiehet es aus, als würde die Bibel Lügen geſtraft. Es ſieht aus, als hätte Gott die Bauern und Handwerker am 5ten Tage, und die Fürſten und Großen am 6ten gemacht, und als hätte der Herr zu dieſen geſagt: Herrſchet über alles Gethier, das auf Erden kriecht, und hätte die Bauern und Bürger zum Gewürm gezählt. Das Leben der Fürſten iſt ein langer Sonntag; das Volk aber liegt vor ihnen wie Dünger auf dem Acker. Der Bauer geht hinter dem Pflug, der Beamte des Fürſten geht aber hinter dem Bauer und treibt ihn mit den Ochſen am Pflug; der Fürſt nimmt das Korn und läßt dem Volke die Stoppeln. Das Leben des Bauern iſt ein langer Werktag; Fremde verzehren ſeine Äcker vor ſeinen Augen, ſein Leib iſt eine Schwiele, ſein Schweiß iſt das Salz auf dem Tiſche des Zwingherrn.

Im Großherzogthum Heſſen ſind 718,373 Einwohner, die geben an den Staat jährlich an 6,363,364 Gulden, als

| | | |
|---|---|---|
| 1) Direkte Steuern | 2,128,131 fl. | |
| 2) Indirekte Steuern | 2,478,264 | „ |
| 3) Domänen | 1,547,394 | „ |
| 4) Regalien | 46,938 | „ |
| 5) Geldſtrafen | 98,511 | „ |
| 6) Verſchiedene Quellen | 64,[...] | „ |
| | 6,363,364 fl. | |

Dies Geld iſt der Blutzehnte, der von dem Leib des Volks genommen wird. An 700,000 Menſchen ſchwitzen, ſtöhnen und hungern dafür. Im Namen des Staates wird es erpreßt, die Preſſer berufen ſich auf die Regierung und die Regierung ſagt, das ſey nöthig, die Ordnung im Staat zu erhalten. Was iſt denn nun das für gewaltiges Ding: der Staat? Wohnt eine Anzahl Menſchen in einem Land und es ſind Verordnungen oder Geſetze vorhanden, nach denen ein jeder ſich richten muß, ſo ſagt man, ſie bilden einen Staat. Der Staat alſo ſind Alle; die Ordner im Staate ſind die Geſetze, durch welche das Wohl Aller geſichert wird, und die aus dem Wohl Aller hervorgehen ſollen. — Seht nun, was man in dem Großherzogthum aus dem Staat gemacht hat; ſeht was es heißt: die Ordnung im Staate erhalten! 700,000 Menſchen bezahlen dafür 6 Millionen, d. h. ſie werden zu Ackergäulen und Pflugſtieren gemacht, damit ſie in Ordnung leben. In Ordnung leben heißt hungern und geſchunden werden.

Wer ſind denn die, welche dieſe Ordnung gemacht haben, und die wachen, dieſe Ordnung zu erhalten? Das iſt die Großherzogliche Regierung. Die Regierung wird gebildet von dem Großherzog und ſeinen oberſten Beamten. Die andern Beamten ſind Männer, die von der Regierung berufen werden, um jene Ordnung in Kraft zu erhalten. Ihre Anzahl iſt Legion: Staatsräthe und Regierungsräthe, Landräthe und Kreisräthe, Geiſtliche Räthe und Schulräthe, Finanzräthe

261  *Hans Burgkmair, Disputation*    262  *Georg Büchner, "The Hessian Messenger"*    263  *Scene from Schiller's drama "The Robbers"*

# The freedom of art made it possible to comprehend the reality of the world in images,

264 *Albrecht Dürer, "The four riders of the Apocalypse"*

265 *Wolf Huber, "Bridge in the Mountains"*

ALEXANDER·M·DARIVM·VLT·SVPERAT
CÆSIS·IN·ACIE·PERSAR·PEDIT·CM·EQVIT
VERO·A·M·INTERFECTIS·MATRE·QVOQVE
CONIVGE·LIBERIS·DARII·REGIS·CVM·M·HAVD
AMPLIVS·EQVITIB·FVGA·DILAPSI·CAPTIS·

266
*Albrecht Altdorfer,*
*Battle of Issus*

267 *Wilhelm von Hirsau's astrolabe*

268 *Room in Keppler's house in Regensburg*

174

# in words and knowledge

272  *Johann Sebastian Bach*

273  *Immanuel Kant*

*274  Johann Wolfgang von Goethe*

*275  Georg Wilhelm Friedrich Hegel*

276  *Friedrich Schiller*     277  *Georg Büchner*     278  *Heinrich Heine*

279  *Schiller's birthplace at Marbach on the Neckar*

*280  Johann Gottlieb Fichte*        *281  Alexander von Humboldt*        *282  Ludwig van Beethoven*

*283  Beethoven's birthplace at Bonn*

*284   Caspar David Friedrich, "Two Men Contemplating the Moon"*

285  *Jacob and Wilhelm Grimm*    286  *Joseph, Baron von Eichendorff*    287  *Neuschwanstein castle*    181

288 *Carl Spitzweg, "The Stork's Arrival"*

289 *Robert Schumann*

290 *An evening with Ludwig Tieck*

Ein Abend bei Ludwig Tieck.

291  *Carl Maria von Weber*

292  *Felix Mendelssohn-Bartholdy*

293  *Johannes Brahms*

294  *Richard Wagner, "Tristan und Isolde"*

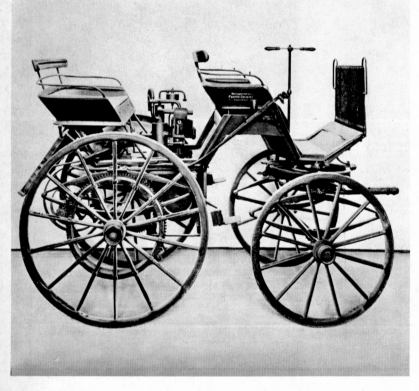

295  Karl Marx

296  Rudolf Diesel

297  Paul Ehrlich

298  Daimler car

299  Johann Philipp Reis

above: *300 Robert Koch* *301 Albert Einstein* *302 Wilhelm Conrad Röntgen* below: *303 Werner von Siemens* *304 The air ship "Zeppelin"*

**Germany Today**

Partner of the nations

Questioned authority

Evolutionary society

Committing others

314  *John F. Kennedy, Frankfurt 1963*

315  *Hamburg – old and new*

316  *Werner Heisenberg*

317  *A development aid helper in India*

# Freetime–Freedom?

## Integrated
## Nationality
## Internationality

## Divided,
## not separated

*318   On the beach*

*319   NATO generals*

*320   Berlin, Brandenburg gate*

"I swear to devote my strength to the welfare
of the German people,
to increase its benefits,
to deflect harm from it,
to preserve and defend
the Basic Law and the Federal Laws,
to fulfil my duties conscientiously
and to practise justice to everyone.
So help me God."

*321  Theodor Heuss, President 1949–1959*

322  *Heinrich Lübke, President 1959–1969*     323  *Gustav Heinemann, President since 1969*

# Partner of the nations

324  *S. Truman and G. C. Marshall discussing "Marshall Plan" aid*

325  *Signing of the Treaty of Rome, Rome 1957*

326  *Charles de Gaulle and Konrad Adenauer, 1962*

327  *Habib Bourgiba and Ludwig Erhard, Bonn 1966*

328  *Nikolai Bulganin, Konrad Adenauer, Nikita Chrustchov, Moscow 1955*

329  *Georges Pompidou, Kurt Georg Kiesinger, 1969*

330  *Willy Brandt, Queen Elizabeth II, 1970*

331  *Gustav Heinemann, Amsterdam 1969*

*332  Nelly Sachs, holder of the German Book Trade Peace Prize 1965*

333  *IV documenta, Kassel 1968*    199

through art and culture

334 *The award of the Nobel Prize for Medicine to Feodor Lynen, Stockholm 1964*

335 *Gustaf Gründgens, Boris Pasternak, Moscow 1959*

336 *World Cup, Germany versus*
*Hungary, Berne 1954*

337 *The "Germany Eight",*
*Olympic Games, Mexico 1968*

339  *Kurt Georg Kiesinger,*
     *Hans Filbinger,*
     *Christian Democratic Party*
     *Conference (CDU)*

340  *Franz Josef Strauß,*
     *chairman of the*
     *Christian Socialist Union (CSU)*

341  *Hildegard Hamm-Brücher,*
     *Walter Scheel,*
     *Ralf Dahrendorf,*
     *leading members of the*
     *Free Democratic Party (FDP)*

342  *Karl Schiller (SPD),*
     *Federal Minister for Economics*

*Parliamentary party leaders*

343  *Wolfgang Mischnik, FDP*

344  *Rainer Barzel, CDU/CSU*

345]  *Herbert Wehner, SPD*

# Informing the public

346 *Ralf Dahrendorf,*
*Sociologist,*
*member of the*
*European Community*
*Commission*
*in Brussels*

47 *Willy Brandt during*
*the elections in 1969*

348  *Willy Brandt, Federal Chancellor*

349  *Walter Scheel, Vice-Chancellor and Foreign Minister*

# Controlled temporary power:

*350  Kai-Uwe von Hassel, Speaker of the German Federal Parliament*     *351  Carlo Schmid, Deputy Speaker of the German Federal Parliament*

*352  Rudolf Augstein, editor of the news magazine "Der Spiegel"*     *353  Günter Grass, author of "The Tin Drum"*

# Germany today:

*354–356  Country family*

357–359  *Town family*                    211

# Life from tradition and progress

360   *Ulm, the old part of the city*

361 Neu-Ulm,
*modern
architecture*

# Democratic Education

# Publicly advised, parents determine the upbringing and training of their children

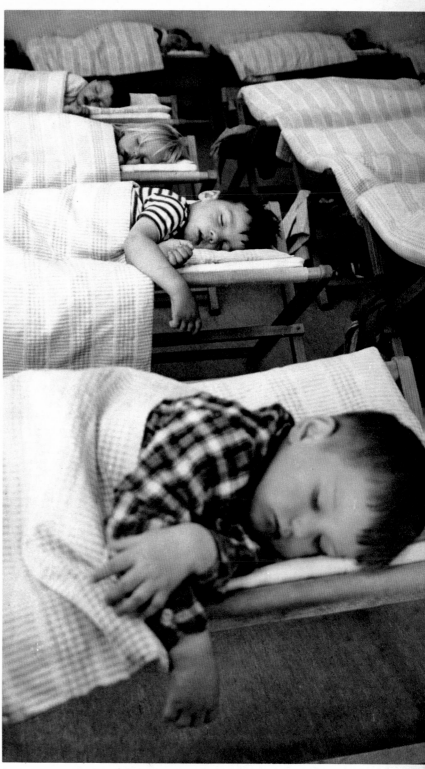

overleaf: *366 School in Frankfurt-on-Main* 215

# Equal educational

367  *Road-safety instruction*

368  *Calculating machines in class*

369  *Language laboratory*

370 *Television in school*

371 *Woodwork class*

372 *Youth engaged in research* 219

*373  Instructional course at evening school*

374   *Machines for the deaf*

375   *Painting class*

# the young generation

*378 Overcrowded universities*

379  *Alexander Mitscherlich, social psychologist, winner of the Peace Prize awarded by the German Book Trade*          380  *In the lecture hall*          227

*381   Wolfgang Leonhard, politologist*                          *382   Rudolf Mössbauer, Nobel prize winner for Physics, 1961*

383 *University seminary*

Protest: demanded reform of university and society

*385  Herbert Marcuse, Free University of Berlin, 1968*          *386  Rudi Dutschke and Ralf Dahrendorf, 1968*

*387 Demonstration*

*388  Student help for Florence following the flood catastrophe in 1966*   235

Between pulpit and protest

# Between pulpit and protest

236

*391 Stained glass window in church by H. G. von Stockhausen*

*393–394  Catholic church conference in Essen, 1968:    address by Cardinal Frings; Final ceremony*

overleaf:   *395  The radar and satellite tracking station in Raisting near Munich*

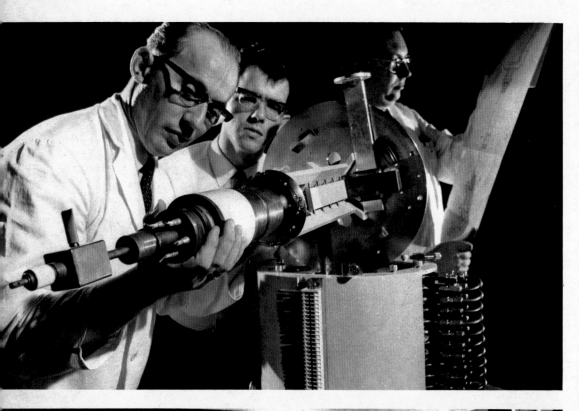

396 *High capacity valves for use in the communications network via earth satellites*    397 *Computers*

398  *Testing antennae under space conditions*

399 *Chemist
analysing foodstuffs*

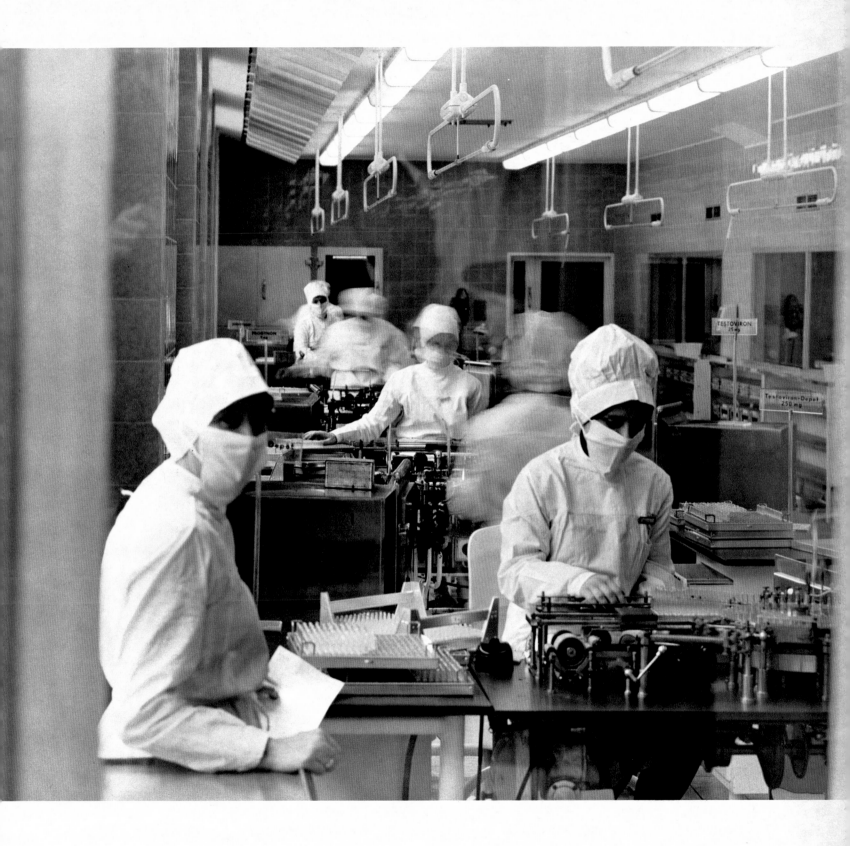

Long-term structural planning, modern machines:

*408  Count Pocci, farmer*

*409  Josef Ertl, Federal Minister for Food, Agriculture and Forestry*

410  *Count Bernadotte, gardener and farmer*    251

# Community and individual responsibility:

*413  Smelting plant in Rheinhausen*

*414  Lignite surface workings near Cologne*     overleaf:  *415  The Severin bridge, Cologne*     255

*416 Assembly line*                                          *417 Hamburg harbour*

418 *Traffic filter*

419  *Clover leaf intersection on the Autobahn near Walldorf*     overleaf:  *420  Hamburg harbour*

*421  Construction of a steel works in India*

422 German
Agricultural
Exhibition
in India

423 Large power
station
in Argentina

INDUSTRIALISIERUNG GEDEIHEN

424 *State visit of*
*President Lübke*
*to the Cameroons*
*in 1966*

425 *Power station in Brazil*

266

# Travelling overcomes frontiers and prejudices

427  *School-party travel*

428  *International holiday camp*

429  *Hunting*

430  *A walk in the snow*

433 *Carnival celebrations in Munich*

431 *A session of the club "Schlaraffia"*

432 *An address from the "barrel"*

434 *Franz Beckenbauer (centre), Czelko Perusič (right)*

435  *Gerd Müller (centre, standing), king of the goal-scorers*  273

437  *Pigeon fanciers*                    438  *Stamp collectors*    **275**

439 *Hikers*

440 *Motor racing
at the Nürburgring*

441 *Horse racing–
western style*

overleaf:

442 *Crowd listening
to John F. Kennedy's
speech in Berlin, 1963*

277

443  *The Federal President, Theodor Heuss, during the state visit to Britain in 1958*

444  *Konrad Adenauer and Lyndon B. Johnson, U.S.A., 1961*     445  *Heinrich Lübk*

446 *Statesmen of many nations in Bonn on the occasion of Konrad Adenauer's funeral in 1967*

447  Richard Nixon
     and Willy Brandt 1967

448  King Hussein of Jordan and
     Kurt Georg Kiesinger, 1967

449  *Kurt Georg Kiesinger
with Fedor Zarapkin,
Soviet Ambassador
to the Federal
Republic, 1969*

450  *Willy Brandt
with Jon G. Maurer,
prime minister
of Romania, 1969*

451 *Nato manoevres*

*453   Fedor Zarapkin, Soviet Ambassador to the Federal Republic, Nikolai S. Patolitchev, Foreign Trade Minister, and Karl Schiller at the Hanover Trade Fair*

455 Motor Show,
Frankfurt 1967

456 Food Exhibition,
Cologne 1967

457   *International Book Fair, Frankfurt. The award of the Peace Prize to the Indian statesman Sarvepalli Radhakrishnan, 1961*   289

*458   A meeting of authors "Group 47"*

459 The authors
Günter Grass,
Vladimir Semyonov
and Uwe Jonson

460 A performance by the
Munich political
cabaret
"Lach- und
Schießgesellschaft"

# Literature

above: *461 Martin Walser   462 Erich Kästner   463 Hans Magnus Enzensberger*   below: *464 Heinrich Böll   465 Gabriele Wohmann   466 Jürgen Becker*

above: *467 Carl Orff 468 Wilhelm Killmayer 469 Werner Egk*    below: *470 Bernd-Alois Zimmermann 471 Hans Werner Henze 472 Nicolaus A. Huber*    293

473 *Performance of "Marat" by Peter Weiss*

474  *Peter Handke, "Kaspar"*     475  *Tankred Dorst, "Toller"*     476  *J. W. von Goethe, "Torquato Tasso"*     295

# Concert, Ballet and Opera

478  *Igor Stravinsky, Hamburg 1958*

480  *Hans Rosbaud, Pierre Boulez, Donaueschingen 1958*

479  *Karlheinz Stockhausen, Darmstadt 1957*

481  *The Berlin "Philharmonie"*

overleaf:    *482  Lynn Seymour, ballet of the German Opera, Berlin*

*483  Marcia Haydee, Württemberg State Ballet, Stuttgart*    299

484  *Anja Silja as "Lulu"*
     *(Wedekind/Alban Berg)*

485  *Bernd-Alois Zimmermann,*
     *"The Soldiers"*

486  *Krystoff Penderecki,*
     *"The Devils of Loudon"*

*487  Peter Lilienthal, "Tramp"*     *488  Peter Zadek, Tankred Dorst, "Rotmord"*

490 *E. W. Nay*                  491 *Horst Antes*

# Separated, not divided

*493  Berlin, north bend of the municipal motor way*

494  Berlin, Frederick William Memorial Church

495 *Sport Palace,*
*6-day cycle racing*

496 *Klaus Schütz,*
*governing mayor*

497 *Curio shop*
*"Zillemarkt"*

501 *Europa Center*

498 *Half-timbered house,*
*Spandau*

499 *Schiller Theatre:*
*Samuel Beckett*
*and Martin Held*
*during the rehearsal of*
*"The Last Tape"*

502 *The Wannsee*

500 *"Leierorje"*
*(barrel organ)*

*503* »*Unter den Linden*«, *East Berlin*        *504  Karl Marx Avenue, East Berlin*        *505  Frontier check-point between East and West Berlin*        3¹3

# Cultural meeting-point Berlin

above:  *506  Fritz Kortner   507  Hans Uhlmann*    below:  *508  Hans Scharoun   509  Erwin Piscator*

above:   *510   Heinz Trökes*     *511   Boris Blacher*     *512   Jule Hammer*

below:   *513   Hildegard Knef*     *514   Helene Weigel*     *515   Walter Höllerer*             overleaf:   *516   Berlin-Center by night*     315

## The photographs used for the dust cover were supplied by:

Bauhaus-Archiv, Darmstadt (1), Landesbildstelle Berlin (1), Bayer. Flugdienst H. Bertram, München (1: Freigabe BStfWuV G 4, Nr. 2/29), Bildarchiv Bruckmann, München (1), H. Busch, Frankfurt (1), Deutsches Institut für Filmkunde, Wiesbaden (1), M. Friedel, München (1), R. Häusser, Mannheim (1), F. Hartung, Saarbrücken (1), Th. Höpker, München (1), H. Hubmann, Ambach (2), St. Moses, München (2), H. Pabel, Grafing (1), Luftbild M. Prugger, München (1: Freigabe BStMWV G 30/133), W. Rauh, Bayreuth (1), Rheinisches Bildarchiv Köln (1), K. de Riese, München (1), Römisch-Germanisches Zentralmuseum, Mainz (1), H. Saebens, Worpswede (1), R. Siegel, Breckerfeld (1), K. Schmitt, Biedenkopf (1), Bildarchiv der Staatsbibliothek Preußischer Kulturbesitz, Berlin (1), Bilderdienst Süddeutscher Verlag, München (3), Ullstein-Bilderdienst (1), Werkfoto VW, Wolfsburg (1).

## Plates in the illustrated section. The figures in italics correspond in each case to the plate numbers.

Archiv E. Angenendt, Herdecke *25*; Archiv der Brüder Unität, Herrnhut *121*; Badisches Landesmuseum Karlsruhe *137*, *216*; D. Bartcky, Frankfurt *18*; Werkfoto BASF *79*, *182*; Bauhaus Archiv, Darmstadt *66*, *311*; Bavaria-Verlag München *140* (H. Teuffen); Werkfoto Bayer *26*; Bayer. Flugdienst H. Bertram, München *2*: Freigabe BStfWuV G 4, Nr. 2/29; Bayerische Staatsbibliothek, München *103*; R. Betz, München *263*, *485*; Foto-Bitter *204*; Foto-Blau, Bonn *185*; Bodelschwingh-Archiv, Bethel *118*; V. Böckstiegel, Werther *117*; Bildarchiv Bruckmann, München *51*, *91*, *100*, *109–111*, *113*, *114*, *120*, *142*, *179*, *187*, *220*, *232*, *251*, *264*, *266*, *273*, *274*, *276*, *278*, *282*, *286*, *288*, *289*, *291–293*; Luftbild A. Brugger, Stuttgart *13*, *29*, *99*, *184*: Freigeg. v. Innenminist. Baden-Württemberg, Nr. 2/16395, Nr. 2/15072, Nr. 2/21374, Nr. 2/15469; I. Buhs, Berlin *499*; Bund deutscher Konsumgenossenschaften, Hamburg *197*; Bundesbildstelle, Bonn *43*, *57*, *60*, *62*, *78*, *141*, *144*, *172*, *175*, *207*, *208*, *223*, *224*, *230*, *233*, *234*, *246*, *280*, *299*, *300*, *313*, *321–323*, *325*, *329–331*, *447–449*; Bildarchiv des Bundesverkehrsministeriums, Bonn *27*; H. Busch, Frankfurt *147*, *151*, *211*, *219*; W. Castelli, Lübeck *131*, *165*, *170*; H. Claassen, Köln *242*; J. H. Darchinger, Bonn *194*, *195*; Deutsche Fotothek, Dresden *134*, *284*; Deutsche Zentrale für Fremdenverkehr, Frankfurt *108*; Deutsche Bundesbahn *243*; Deutsches Institut für Filmkunde, Wiesbaden *309*; Deutsches Museum, München *298*; J. Diederichs, Berlin *193*; T. Dorst, München *488*; dpa *63–65*, *68*, *71*, *173*, *241*, *244*, *245*, *332*, *334*, *337*, *343–345*, *445*, *453*, *457*, *473*; Ö. Ertogan, Bonn *198*; Eternit *401*; G.Fehr, Bonn *148*; Film-Bild- und Tonbandstelle, Bonn *28*; Foto Marburg, Marburg *47*, *48*, *130*; K. D. Francke, Hamburg *54*, *95*; Historisches Museum, Stadtarchiv Frankfurt *155*, *171*; Historia-Foto Ch. Fremke, Bad Sachsa *143*, *189*, *277*; M. Friedel, München *354*, *355*, *357*, *358*, *362*, *365*, *372*, *376*, *410*, *441*; Germanisches Nationalmuseum Nürnberg *102*, *160*; Photographie Giraudon, Paris *36*; R. Gööck, Bachmühle *249*; F. Götz, Radolfzell *82*, *85*; Foto-Graeber, Marbach *279*; Grigutsch, Bonn *76*, E. Groth-Schmachtenberger, München *101*; Photo-Gundermann, Würzburg *225*; N. Haas, Trier *39*, *254*; E. W. Haase, Hamburg *10*; H.-W. Hämer, Berlin *477*; R. Häusser, Mannheim *9*, *24*, *53*, *80*, *259*; W. Hassenstein *201*; F. Hartung, Saarbrücken *336*; Haude & Spenersche Verlagsbuchhandlung, Berlin *199*; M. Hauschild, Hannover *252*; F. & E. Heimhuber, Sonthofen *12*; H. Held, Köln *46*; R. Henneberger, München *58*; Foto-Herpach, München *287*; Herzog-Anton-Ulrich-Museum, Braunschweig *154*; Historisches Museum Hanau *40*; Th. Höpker, München *315*, *319*, *341*, *346*, *348*, *377*, *386*, *399*, *411*, *412*, *417*, *424*, *450*, *451*, *452*; Zeitgeschichtliches Bildarchiv Heinrich Hofmann, München *237*; R. Holtappel, Oberhausen *474*; Photo-Holtmann, Stuttgart *8*, *20*, *21*, *210*; Sammlung F. Hottenroth, München *145*; H. Hubmann, Ambach *176*, *317*, *326*, *328*, *421*, *444*; Inst. f. Weltraumforschung, Bochum *1*; Inter Nationes, Bonn-Bad Godesberg *119*, *281*; M. Jacoby, Berlin *442*, *493–495*, *497*, *501*, *516*; J. Jeiter, Hadamar *4*, *55*, *88*, *127*, *128*, *158*, *174*, *385*; L. Kaster, Gruiten *209*; KNA, Frankfurt *123*; G. Kerff, Hamburg *6*; Keystone Pressedienst *70*, *191*, *192*, *414*, *478*; H. Kilian, Stuttgart *482*, *483*; Pressebilderdienst Kindermann, Berlin *487*; H. Kinkel, Stuttgart *491*; Bildarchiv F. Klee, Bern *307*; Foto-Kleinfeld, Tübingen *112*; Staatsarchiv Koblenz *42*; laenderpress, Düsseldorf *96*; Landesbildstelle Berlin *226*, *227*, *496*, *498*, *504*; Landesbildstelle Rheinland, Düsseldorf *81*, *94*; Landesbildstelle Westfalen, Münster *149*; Landesbildstelle Württemberg, Stuttgart *5*; Landesmuseum Münster *135*; J. Le Brun, Konstanz *107*; Limes-Verlag, Wiesbaden *115*; H. List, München *506–508*, *510*, *512*, *514*, *515*; P. Ludwig, Darmstadt *479*; D. Meller-Marcovic, München *122*, *351*, *352*; L. Mory, München *162*; St. Moses, München *316*, *318*, *320*, *340*, *342*, *347*, *349*, *350*, *353*, *359*, *364*, *379*, *380*, *387*, *393*, *394*, *408*, *420*, *428*, *430–433*, *437*, *439*, *458*, *463*, *469*, *490*, *500*, *505*, *509*; E. Müller, Kassel *217*; A. Münchow, Aachen *34*; Staatsarchiv Münster *124*; R. Neumann, München *382*; W. Neumeister, München *11*, *17*, *35*, *56*, *89*, *90*, *132*, *146*, *153*, *156*, *164*, *181*, *214*, *215*, *222*, *268*, *400*; H. Nölter, Hannover *180*; Hauptamt für Hochbauwesen, Nürnberg *159*, *161*, *167*; St. Odry, Köln-Ehrenfels *470*; Bildarchiv der Österreichischen Nationalbibliothek, Wien *290*; Hilmar Pabel, Grafing *335*; H. Paulmann, Bonn *231*; Petersen, Bonn *283*; Sammlung Pick, München *206*; W. Pragher, Freiburg *97*; Presse- und Informationsamt Berlin *502*, *503* (beide Uwe Rau, Berlin); Luftbild M. Prugger, München *178*: Freigabe BStMWV G 30/133, *338*; W. Rauh, Bayreuth *138*, *294*; G. R. Reitz, Hannover *426*; Renziehausen, Heide *87*; Rheinisches Bildarchiv, Köln *52*, *168*; Rheinisches Landesmuseum Bonn *19*, *31*, *33*, *49*; L. Richter, Mainz *269*; K. de Riese, München *333*, *360*, *361*, **366**, *369–371*, *374*, *375*, *378*, *381*, *383*, *384*, *388–392*, *395*, *397*, *398*, *409*, *427*, *436*, *461*, *465–468*, *471*, *472*, *489*, *492*; roebild *3*, *253* (beide H. Busch, Frankfurt); Römisch-Germanisches Zentralmuseum Mainz *16*; I. v. d. Ropp, Rodenkirchen *177*; H. Saebens, Worpswede *22*, *23*, *129*, *139*, *150*; M. Scheler, Hamburg *418*, *429*; W. Schiffer, Bensberg-Refrath *356*, *402–407*; Historischer Bilderdienst E. Schlee, Berlin *250*; Schleswig-Holsteinisches Landesmuseum für Vor- und Frühgeschichte, Schleswig *32*; H. Schmidt-Glassner, Stuttgart *37*, *126*, *166*, *213*, *218*, *257*; K. Schmitt, Biedenkopf *93*; Foto-Schmölz, Köln *136*; T. Schneiders, Lindau *7*, *415*; W. Schröder, Frankfurt *61*; Service de Presse et d'Information des Communautées Européennes *247*; R. Siegel, Breckerfeld *84*; Siemens Pressebild *75*, *205*, *303*, *367*, *425*; W. Spitta, Burgweinting *38*, *50*, *106*, *125*, *152*, *267*; Staatliche Graphische Sammlungen, München *261*, *265*, *285*; Bildarchiv der Staatsbibliothek Preußischer Kulturbesitz, Berlin *44*, *105*, *186*, *258*, *260*, *262*, *270–272*, *275*, *295*, *297*, *304*; H.Stahl, Köln *77*; W. Steinkopf, Berlin *83*, *104*, *228*; H. Steinmetz, Gräfelfing *200*; G. Stoletzki, Wolfenbüttel *116*; Luftbild D. Storp, Düsseldorf *14*: Freigeg. Reg.-Präs. Düsseldorf Nr. D. St. *1293*, *413*; A.Storz, Stuttgart *229*; Luftbild Strähle, Schorndorf *15*; Bilderdienst Südd. Verlag, München *30*, *69*, *188*, *196* (AP), *236*, *296*, *305*, *312* (dpa), *324* (AP), *327* (Upi), *339*, *363*, *368* (Keystone), *373* (F.Neuwirth, München), *396* (Siemens,) *416*, *422* (dpa), *438* (H. List, München), *440* (AP), *446* (dpa), *454* (F. Raith, München), *455* (AP), *456* (F. Neuwirth, München), *459* (H. O. Jurisch, Berlin), *460* (AP), *462* (AP), *480*, *481* (AP), *511* (F. Eschen, Berlin), *513* (K. P. A., Düsseldorf); P. Swiridoff, Schwäbisch Hall *157*, *464*; H. Teuffen, Neufahrn *92*, *239*; F. Thorbecke, Lindau *419*; Toledo Museum of Art, Toledo (Ohio) *133*; K. Treutwein, Schweinfurt *86*; Ullstein-Bilderdienst *59*, *67*, *72–74*, *183*, *235*, *238*, *240*, *255*, *301*, *302*, *306*, *308*, *310*, *314*, *443* (AP); Stadtarchiv Ulm *169*; Ulmer Museum *163*; Universitätsbibliothek Heidelberg *212*, *256*; Kraftwerk Union, Erlangen *423*; Sammlung Vellguth, Bonn-Bad Godesberg *248*; Verlag Velhagen & Klasing, Berlin *221*; Günther Vierow, Bremen *476*; K.-H. Völker, Viermünden *41*; Werkfoto VW, Wolfsburg *202*; Foto-WEREK, München *434*, *435*; Wermeling, Nienberge *98*; L. Windstoßer, Stuttgart *203*; M. Winkler-Betzendahl, Stuttgart *475*, *484*, *486*.

The quotations by Prodosh Aich, Pura Santillan Castrence, Albert Joh. Marie van Dal, Peter Dürrenmatt, Johannes Gaitanides, Agne Hamrin, Kazuo Kani, Stefan Kisielewski, Horacio G. Lebrón, Terence Prittie, Pietro Quaroni, Flavien Ranaivo, Léopold Sédar Senghor have been taken in condensed form from the book "Sind die Deutschen wirklich so?" ("Are Germans really like this?") by Hermann Ziok (Horst-Erdmann-Verlag, Tübingen).

## Structures – Land of encounter

1 *Germany in the heart of Europe:* Radio photograph via the USA weather satellite "ESSA 2", taken from a height of 900 miles.

2 *The Zugspitze massif near Garmisch-Partenkirchen:* Germany's share of the northern chalk alps are the Allgäu alps, the Wetterstein range with the Zugspitze (9,724 feet) the Karwendel and the Berchtesgaden alps.

3 *Red cliffs of the island of Sylt:* The largest North Friesian island off the west coast of Schleswig-Holstein.

4 *The Rhine near Bacharach:* Between Mainz and Bonn the Rhine (total length 820 miles, of which 430 miles is within Germany) flows through one of the great European landscapes, renowned for its castles and wine centres, of which Bacharach is one of the oldest; together with the four neighbouring wine-producing valleys, Bacharach was granted municipal freedom as early as the 13th century. Total annual traffic on the Rhine – 130 to 150 million tons.

5 *The Danube near Werenwag Castle:* In its upper reaches the Danube cuts through the Schwäbische Alb (Swabian Jura).

6 *The Elbe near Blankenese* below Hamburg. According to the volume of traffic the Elbe (length 720 miles) is of utmost importance both for Germany and Czechoslovakia, since it is navigable well inside Bohemia.

7 *A beechwood forest in the Spessart* between Frankfurt and Würzburg.

8 *Southern part of the Black Forest:* The Black Forest is, with the Feldberg (4,898 feet), the highest range of the Central Uplands in Southern Germany; it follows the Rhine for a length of a round 100 miles. On the higher slopes, the mixed variety of trees gives way to white fir and pine.

9 *Palatinate forest and Trifels Castle,* in which Richard the Lionheart was held prisoner 1193/94. From 1195 to the end of the 13th century the castle was used for the safe-keeping of imperial jewels.

10 *Lüneburg Heath:* see remarks on illustration 18.

11 *Volcanic lake* in the Eifel near Daun, created like other similar lakes by a volcanic explosion of gas.

12 *Höfats in the Allgäu:* The slopes of the Höfats consist of very soft, badly weather-beaten sand and limestone and are famous for their particularly luxuriant flora.

13 *Nördlingen* in the centre of a fertile basin (known as "Ries") which was created 15 million years ago by a falling meteorite. The city of this former Free Imperial City, with its 16 towers, still remains intact today.

14 *Duisburg:* Rhenish commercial centre on both sides of the Ruhr estuary. Half destroyed in World War II, Duisburg is the largest inland port in the world and one of the centres of the Ruhr industry.

15 *Ehrenfels Castle* in the Rhine Valley at the entrance to the "Binger Loch", customs house and place of safekeeping for Mainz Cathedral's treasures. The terrace-shaped vineyards on the slopes of the Niederwald are amongst the oldest in the Rhine Valley.

16 *Franconian ornamental disc* from Dolsheim, Germano-Roman Museum in Mainz. The decorative discs, found in numerous Franconian graves and about 3–4 inches in diameter, were used as decoration on leather pouches and as belt pendants.

17 *Lake dwellings in Unteruhldingen on Lake Constance:* The lake-dwellers' village reconstructed in Unteruhldingen near Meersburg and dating from 3/2,000 BC was found in the Feder Lake in Swabia.

18 *Cairns on the Lüneburg Heath:* With an area of about 440 square miles, the largest heath in Germany. The gigantic stone graves belong to the Megalithic Age, 5/3,000 BC, which, it has been established, existed throughout Europe.

19 *Foundations of a Roman villa in Liblar:* Aerial photograph of a Roman villa from about AD 200 near Euskirchen in the Rhineland. For the purposes of aerial archeology, the outline of the walls concealed beneath the surface has been made recognisable by discolouring the plants.

20 *Traditional costume of Mühlenbach* in the Black Forest.

21 *Black Forest farmhouse:* In the Black Forest the "single building" is
22 predominant. In contrast to the *Frisian houses,* where the cattle and farm are to be found without separating walls around the barn area, with the Black Forest house, living quarters, stable and barn are built one behind the other.

23 *Traditional costume of Lindhorst near Bückeburg* in Schaumburg-Lippe.

24 *Fields near Lörrach* at the southern tip of the Black Forest.

25 *Rheinhausen,* industrial town on the Lower Rhine, opposite Duisburg.

26 *The Bayer Works:* The plant at Leverkusen, Rhineland, is one of Germany's leading chemical works (pharmaceutical and plant-protecting products, plastics and synthetic fibres).

27 *Frontier check-point on the German/Belgian autobahn near Aachen:* Modern fast highways, like the one shown here, the "Route Baudouin", link the Federal Republic with her neighbours in the West, South and North.

28 *Border between the Federal Republic and the German Democratic Republic near Lauenstein:* 850 miles of barbed-wire fence and minefields on East German territory separate Germans from Germans.

29 *Lake Constance,* second largest lake in Western Europe, between the Federal Republic, Switzerland and Austria, with its numerous towns and monasteries, is a focal point of Western culture. Top right, the island of Mainau, in the background, the Swiss and Austrian alps.

30 *The bridge over the Fehmarn Sound,* a link in the "Vogellinie" (as the crow flies) between Scandinavia and Germany, serving road and rail traffic.

31 *Sandstone pillar from Pfalzfeld:* St. Goar county, probably used to embellish a Celtic burial mound in the earlier Latèn age (about 200 BC). Location: Rhenish State Museum, Bonn.

32 *Runic stone from Haithabu,* an early trading post on the Schlei near Schleswig. The inscription commemorates Sigfrygg, son of King Knuba, who was defeated in AD 934 by the German King Henry I. Location: The Schleswig-Holstein State Museum for the Prehistoric and Early Historic Age, Schleswig.

33 *Franconian gravestone in Niederdollendorf* near Bonn with heathen and early christian themes. Location: Rhenish State Museum, Bonn.

34 *Lothar's Cross,* about AD 1,000 from the treasures of Aachen Cathedral. The Augustinian Cameo is of ancient origin.

35 *The Basilica in Trier* is, together with the Pantheon in Rome, the largest preserved ancient interior (about 167×93 feet long, 100 feet high). Built as a court of justice and throne-room by Emperor Constantine, who lived in Augusta Treverorum (Trier) from AD 306–312.

The brick building, originally coated with stucco and marble, was a royal palace in Frankish times. Restored 1946–56 as a Protestant church.

*36 Otto II receiving homage from the provinces:* Germania, Francia, Italia and Alemania. A page from the Master of the "Registrum Gregorii" (about AD 983, Trier). Today in the Condé Museum in Chantilly.

*37 Royal hall of Lorsch Monastery on the Bergstrasse,* AD 774, served originally as a high court of justice.

*38 Portal of the Scottish St. Jacob's Church in Regensburg.* The monastery was founded in AD 1,090 by Irish Benedictine monks. The decoration on the North portal (about AD 1,190) betrays French or Lombardic influence.

*39 Evangelist symbols* from the Codex 61 of the Cathedral library in Trier. The "Evangeliarium" produced about AD 775 in Trier reveals the strong influence of Irish book-illumination. Of the different scribes, a certain "Thomas" is mentioned by name who was also responsible for the illustrated miniature.

*40 Seven-branched candlestick from a Hebrew manuscript* of the 13th century on permanent loan by the Hanau Historical Museum to the Jewish National Museum in Jerusalem.

*41 Mikwe in Friedberg:* The ritual women's bath in Friedberg, Hesse, dates from the year AD 1,260 and is the best preserved of its kind in Germany. An 85 foot shaft leads to the ground water level.

*42 Henry VII presenting the Jews with the Mosaic Law:* Henry VII of Luxembourg (1308–13) is handing the Jews a parchment scroll with the Law of Moses. Illustration from the Dresden Manuscript of the Code of Old Saxon laws, latter half of the 14th century, nowadays in the City Archives, Coblenz (1 C, No. 1, fol. 24).

*43 Ceiling of a hall of prayer in Horb* in Baden-Württemberg: The wooden dome of the hall of prayer, in a private house, is lavishly embellished with paintings.

*44 Roland slaying a heathen* with his horn Oliphant and handing his glove to St. Michael. Roland, nephew of Charlemagne, became the symbolic figure of the subjection to no one but the emperor of many Free Imperial Cities. The miniature comes from a Stricker manuscript of the latter half of the 14th century in the manuscript section, State Library, Foundation of Prussian Culture, Ms. germ. fol. 623, fol. 22 v. See also plate 150.

*45 Konrad von Altstätten:* From the so-called "Manessische Lieder-handschrift" (Song Manuscript) from the valuable Middle High German Lyrics of the latter half of the 14th century, since 1888 in the Heidelberg University Library. Konrad belonged to the 13th century minnesingers under French influence.

*46 West façade of Cologne Cathedral:* Main work of Gothic architecture from 1248 onwards; choir dedicated in 1322. Following the cessation of construction work in 1560, the extension was continued in 1842 and the building completed in 1880.

*47 Sepulchral plate of Archbishop Peter of Aspelt in Mainz Cathedral:* Peter crowned Ludwig of Bavaria (right) German King and John of Luxembourg (left) King of Bohemia. Until the establishment of the Archbishopric of Prague in 1344, the Bohemian provinces were subject to the ecclesiastical sovereignty of the Bishop of Mainz.

*48 Saint Elizabeth helping the poor:* The daughter of the Hungarian King Andreas II married the Landgrave Ludwig of Thuringia; following his early death, she devoted her whole life to the poor. Altar-piece of 1340 from Altenberg Monastery on the Middle Rhine, now in the Städelsche Institute of Art, Frankfurt.

*49 Head of a Bohemian Madonna* from the School of Court Art in Prague under Emperor Charles IV, around 1400; in the Rhenish Land Museum, Bonn.

*50 The Landshut Wedding* held every three years to commemorate the magnificent wedding of the Bavarian Duke George the Rich and Jadwiga of Poland in 1475.

*51 The "Essighaus" in Bremen,* built in 1618 reveals the influence of early Flemish baroque.

*52 St. Mary Magdalene* by Arnt van Tricht from the "Altar of the Holy Trinity", Kalkar, Lower Rhine, completed under strong Dutch influence between 1535–1540.

*53 Heidelberg Castle, Ottheinrich-wing:* The architectural pattern is Italian, the statue-decoration can be traced back to the Dutch sculptors Antonius and Alexander Colin. The German Apothecaries' Museum is to be found on the ground floor.

*56 West façade of Passau Cathedral:* re-built 1668–78 by Carlo Lurago.

*57 Sanssouci Palace, Music room:* Georg Wenzeslaus von Knobelsdorff built this Potsdam summer residence 1745–47 according to Frederick the Great's own plans, of which the music room, decorated by the brothers Joh. Michael und Joh. Christian Hoppenhaupt, ranks amongst the finest rococo rooms in Germany.

*58 Garden façade of Nymphenburg Castle* near Munich, commenced in 1664 by Agosto Barelli and continued to 1728 by Enrico Zuccalli, G. A. Viscardi and Joseph Effner as a summer residence for the Bavarian Electors.

*59 Voltaire and Frederick the Great.* Engraving by P. Beaquoi from a painting by Monsian. Under Voltaire's influence, who lived in Potsdam from 1750–53, Frederick of Prussia became the prototype of enlightened monarchs. He offered asylum to numerous refugees from other countries, particularly to the many Huguenots. At one time, almost a third of the population of Berlin was of French origin; inter alia we

*60* are reminded of this by the *French Cathedral,* built by Gontard in

*62* 1780, in Berlin. Under the banner of religious tolerance, the *mosque in Schwetzingen* near Mannheim was erected. Following the Peace of Münster and Osnabrück, with its articles guaranteeing the tolerance of religious freedom, Germany became the main asylum in the whole of Europe for those persecuted on religious grounds. A late proof of

*61* this tradition of "Liberty" is the *Russian Chapel in Darmstadt* built by Tsar Nicholas II in 1898/99 and which reflects the close affinity of the leading nobility in Germany and Russia in the 19th century.

*63* The Spanish philosopher and sociologist *José Ortega y Gasset* (1883 to 1955) became acquainted with, inter alia, the thoughts of Hegel, Nietzsche and Dilthey and was influenced by the ideas of modern Kantism.

*64 Benedetto Croce* (1866–1952), the outstanding Italian cultural and historical philosopher, remained, because of his studies, closely bound with German intellectual life, and made a fundamental contribution to the international propagation of German idealism.

*65* Around the great German scholar *Max Born* (1882–1970), who emigrated in 1923, gathered in Göttingen between 1923–30 many outstanding foreign atomic physicists, among whom were the Ameri-

68 cans *J. Robert Oppenheimer* (1906–67), Edward Teller and Eugene P. Wigner, the Englishman Paul Dirac, the Italian Enrico Fermi and the Austrian Wolfgang Pauli.

69 *Florence Nightingale* (1820–1910), famous for her care of the wounded in the Crimean War and for founding English nurses' schools, spent some years of her nurse's training in the well-known Deaconess's House in Kaiserswerth.

70 The great Russian writer *Feodor Dostoyevsky* (1821–81) stayed at various times in Germany, inter alia in Dresden and Baden-Baden,

71 and Vladimir Ilyitch Ulyanov, known as *Lenin* (1870–1924), spent two years in Munich as editor of the magazine "Iskra".

66 The Belgian architect *Henry von de Velde* (1863–1957) exercised great influence on the German Crafts Association whilst teaching at the

67 Seminary for Arts and Crafts in Weimar (1912–14). *Igor Stravinsky* (born 1882) composed at the end of the Fifties his work "Threni" on behalf of the North German Radio and conducted some of his own compositions at the Donaueschingen Music Festival in 1967 and the Berlin Festival in 1961 and 1964.

72 *Edvard Munch* (1863–1944), Norwegian painter and artist, representative of the "Jugendstil" (Art Nouveau) and pioneer of the Expressionist Movement, lived for many years in Germany, mainly in

73 Berlin and Lübeck. The American *Lyonel Feininger* (1871–1956) was associated with the Artists' Community "Blaue Reiter", founded in 1911, and was also a teacher at the famous "Bauhaus" between the

74 years 1919–33. The Norwegian illustrator and cartoonist *Olaf Gulbransson* (1873–1958) became an associate of the satirical magazine "Simplicissimus" in Munich and from 1929 was Professor at the Academy for Liberal Arts.

75–80 *Trainees, foreign workers, students* from every corner of the world are learning and working in Germany. In 1970 the foreign workers in the Federal Republic numbered some 1.7 million.

81 *Portraits of burghers* on the high altar of the Collegiate Church of St. Victor in Xanten. The Cologne painter, Barthel Bruyn (1493 – 1555) the Elder, who came from Wesel, portrayed faithfully in the wake of St. Victor and St. Helen, canons, mayors, aldermen and distinguished ladies of Xanten. The panels originate from the year 1534.

82 *Vergil of Strasbourg, Peasants Ploughing.* Woodcut of the first imprint of a Vergil translation, Strasbourg 1468.

83 *Albrecht Dürer, Wire Mill.* Water colour of 1494 now in the Engraving Cabinet of the State Museum, Prussian Cultural Property, Berlin. See Plate 264.

84 *Half-timbered house in Freudenberg, Hesse.* The half-timbered houses were the usual form of architecture in the Middle Ages: which consisted of a framework of wooden beams with loam or brick walls. Artistic patterns of crossbeams and wall decorations reflect the great variety of art forms.

# Society Yesterday and Today

85 *Rebel peasants taking a knight prisoner.* Woodcut from the year 1525 by Hans Burgkmair. Towards the end of the Middle Ages the peasants rebelled in numerous rural areas of Germany to protect their "old rights" against the growing power of the princes. The German Peasants' War from 1524–25 became the most powerful uprising in German history.

86 *The "Free Imperial Village" of Gochsheim* near Schweinfurt was placed under the patronage of the emperor and enjoyed a certain amount of independence in parish council affairs and minor judicial matters. The Imperial Freedom included the right to self-defence with walls and a tower.

87 *Statue commemorating the victory of the Dithmarschen peasants* over the Danish King John on the 17th February 1500. The peasants of this marshland in West Holstein maintained their Peasants' Republic until modern times.

88 *Freedmen's Court near Kaichen in Hesse*, formerly a meeting place of freemen.

89 *Mask from Elzach.* Artistically carved wooden masks are often worn in carnival processions in the Black Forest and the Alpine foothills of Bavaria. These masks symbolise the expulsion of evil spirits.

90 *St. George's Ride near Traunstein.* On the 23rd April Bavarian farmers in the Alpine foothills celebrate St. George's Day by a mounted procession which has its roots in pre-christian customs.

91 *Bed from Lake Schlier* of 1786 in the Bavarian National Museum, Munich. Furniture from Tölz and Lake Schlier offer some of the finest examples of old Bavarian peasant art.

92 *Head boards in Arnbruck* in the Bavarian Forest. After the corpse has lain on the boards, they are then painted in gay colours and set up, usually in groups, in memory of the dead person, near chapels and crucifixes.

93 *Graffiti in Oberhörl* on a farmhouse.

94 *Westerwald dish* from the 18th century and now in the Hetjens Museum of the Düsseldorf Municipal Art Collection.

95 *Lime blossom festival in Schenklengsfeld* (Hesse).

96 *Hop fields* in the Hallertau, north of Munich. The hops are needed for brewing beer.

97 *Vine-covered slopes on the Tuniberg*, Kaiserstuhl. Winegrowing in the Rhineland was first introduced by the Romans.

98 *Cornfield.* Whereas the average corn yield between 1850 und 1950 was about 18 cwt. per acre, it has risen, in the meantime, to about 22 cwt. per acre.

99 *The Allgäu* in Western Bavaria, following World War I, specialised in dairy farming. A carefully planned industrialization supplemented the development of a well-balanced and secure economy.

100 *St. Bernhard and monks working in the fields.* Panel from the altar of the convent in Zwettl, Austria, by the Augsburg artist Jörg Breu (1475–1537). The Cistercian Order, which was assisted by Bernhard of Clairvaux, pioneered land development in many areas.

101 *Maria Laach Monastery* in the Eifel mountains was founded in AD 1093. This Benedictine abbey became the intellectual centre of the

Catholic liturgical movement. During the Nazi regime, Konrad Adenauer sought refuge here for some time.

102 *Cover of the Echternach Codex* in the German National Museum, Nuremberg. This cover dates from the last quarter of the 10th century and originated in the Trier workshop of Bishop Egbert. It belongs to one of the finest examples of 11th century manuscripts and was presented to the Benedictine Monastery in Echternach by Emperor Otto III.

103 *Initial L from the Codex lat. 4453* in the Bavarian State Library, Munich. The "Evangeliar" of Otto III from the Bamberg Cathedral treasures. Reichenau School, about AD 1000.

104 *Henricus de Alemania giving a lecture* on ethics at the Sorbonne, Paris. A miniature by Laurentius da Voltalina in the engraving collection of the State Museum, Berlin, and dating from the second quarter of the 14th century.

105 *Martin Luther* from an engraving by Lucas Cranach the Elder (1520). Luther, born in 1483 in Eisleben, died in 1546, studied law initially before entering an Augustine monastery in 1505. Through the publication of his theses in Wittenberg in 1517, Luther became the founder of the Reformation; he refused to renounce his teachings at the Imperial Diet of Worms in 1521. He translated the Bible into German.

106 *Seat of Albertus Magnus* in the Regensburg Dominican monastery. This great ecclesiastical teacher (1193–1280) assimilated the knowledge of his time, particularly in theology, philosophy and physics. He taught Thomas Aquinius.

107 *Stucco angel in the monastery church in Zwiefalten on the Danube.* Founded in 1089, Zwiefalten was given its superb Baroque style, between 1738–1765, by J. M. Fischer. J. M. Feichtmayr of Augsburg is the most outstanding of the stucco artists.

108 *Benedictine Monastery in Wiblingen.* The library, 1714–60, is a particularly happy example of Baroque interior decoration.

109 *Gotthold Ephraim Lessing* (1729–1781), the leading exponent of rationalism in German literature, came from a Protestant parsonage. As the creator of later German drama ("Nathan") and of domestic tragedy ("Emilia Galotti") he made an important contribution to the development of civic consciousness in Germany.

110 *Friedrich Hölderlin* (1770–1843) studied Protestant theology in Tübingen. His odes and hymns open up new dimensions of linguistic expression.

111 *Georg Friedrich Wilhelm Hegel* (1770–1831), from 1818 professor of philosophy in Berlin, and the last great systematic figure of German idealism, laid the foundations for political and judicial philosophy and gave decisive impulses to Karl Marx.

112 *The Theological Seminary of Tübingen*, was, for a long time, a fertile bed of intellectual life in southern Germany. Schelling, Hegel, Hölderlin, Mörike and Hauff were some of its pupils.

113 *Friedrich Wilhelm Joseph von Schelling* (1775–1854) is one of the outstanding representatives of philosophic idealism; his system of absolute idealism in spirit and nature, subject and object indistinguishable in the absolute (philosophy of identity) was supplemented after 1841 by a philosophy of living existence (of God) i. e. a philosophy of mythology and revelation.

114 *Friedrich Nietzsche* (1844–1910) was a Protestant parson's son, became, as a philosopher and writer, one of the authoritative cultural critics of the late 19th century.

115 *Gottfried Benn* (1886–1956), lyric poet, dramatist and essayist, belongs to the representatives of Expressionism in modern German literature.

116 *Main church in Wolfenbüttel.* Built in the 17th century as the first Protestant house of God in Germany.

118 *Friedrich von Bodelschwingh* (1831–1910), theologian and Protestant priest, is regarded as the father of the institute for epileptics founded

117 in 1867 in *Bethel near Bielefeld* of which he was in charge from 1872. He combined the nursing homes of the deacons' und deaconnesses' institutes to train male and female nurses; by his efforts Bethel became the largest relief organisation of home mission-work.

119 *Convent of atonement, Dachau*, a former concentration camp. The Carmelite nuns, who live here in accordance with the strict rules of their order, built it themselves. The first prioress was closely associated with the resistance fighters of the 20th July 1944.

120 *Nikolaus, Count of Zinzendorf* (1700–1760), brought up in the pietistical spirit, settled Bohemian Brothers on the Berthelsdorf estate near Dresden and founded thereby the Herrnhut Community.

121 *Herrnhut Community*, a water colour from the year 1753. The communal life of the Brothers is distinguished by a belief in justification based on mercy and by serving one's fellow-man. The village community, by general agreement of all the inhabitants, became a self-contained Protestant settlement.

122 *Protestant Academy, Bad Boll.* In order to make discussion possible between the Christian churches and different sections of the public, numerous academies were founded after 1945. Our photograph shows the Marxist philosopher Ernst Bloch at a conference in Bad Bonn in 1967.

123 *Catholic mission in Africa.* The Protestant and Catholic churches in Germany have, for centuries, considered one of their most important tasks to be the propagation of Christian teaching through practical assistance of fellow-man in schools and hospitals. With their relief organisations "Bread for the World" (Protestant) and "Misereor" (Catholic) they have joined the battle against hunger in the world.

124 This last preserved *document of Charlemagne*, dated 9th May 813, confirms a follower's ownership of a beechwood between Werra and Fulda.

125 *Knights jousting* from the Dollinger Room in Regensburg town hall. This stucco relief from the 13th century was originally in the city palace of the knightly Dollinger family.

126 *Ekkehard and Uta.* Founder figures in the west choir of Naumburg Cathedral (1244–1260).

127 *Eltz Castle* in the Eifel mountains, built between the 12th and 16th century, is one of the finest castles of the Middle Ages and Renaissance in Germany.

128 *Landgrave's choir in the church of St. Elizabeth, Marburg.* Family vault of the Hessian landgraves. The church of St. Elizabeth (1235 to 1250), erected over the grave of St. Elizabeth, is one of the first Gothic churches in Germany.

129 *Moated castle, Gemen in Westphalia.* Typical example of seat of nobility in Westphalia and the northern Rhineland. The main building, which dates from 1411, owes its present appearance to reconstruction work carried out in 1693.

130 *The great refectory of the Teutonic Knights in Marienburg Castle*, the residence of the Grand Master of the Order of Teutonic Knights.

This order, founded in 1190 to fight against unbelievers, was called upon for help in 1226 by Duke Konrad of Masovia against the heathen Prussians and subsequently created a state embracing Prussia, East Pomerania, Danzig, Estonia and East Brandenburg. The Order of Knights was defeated by a combined Polish-Lithuanian army at the Battle of Tannenberg in 1410 and was changed into a secular dukedom. The great 14th century refectory is a superb example of North German Gothic architecture in brick. Half destroyed in 1945, the Marienburg was rebuilt by the Polish State and serves today as a museum.

131  *Relief of Electors*. Door embellishment in Lübeck town hall with idealized portraits of the emperor and the electors, dating from the second half of the 14th century. Through the Golden Bull of Charles IV in 1356 the election of the German emperor was determined by seven electors. This principle of an electoral kingdom was handed on from the time of the migrating tribes and provided the possibility of deposing an incompetent ruler. Apart from the archbishops of Cologne, Mainz and Trier, the Count Palatine, the Duke of Saxony, the Margrave of Brandenburg and the King of Bohemia held the office of imperial elector.

132  *The royal rostrum in Rhens on the Rhine*. From 1273 onwards the electors assembled in the orchard near the Rhine to deliberate on the royal election. Charles IV, who was elected here in 1346, had a stone rostrum built after 1376 instead of the wooden structure which the newly-elected emperor mounted to take possession of the empire symbolically.

133  *Elector Frederick the Wise of Saxony, Martin Luther and Ulrich Zwingli*. Painting by Lucas Cranach the Elder (1472–1553), a friend of Luther. The picture portrays the religious discussion in Marburg in 1529 which led to the two reformers going separate ways. This picture is now in the Toledo Museum of Art, Toledo, Ohio (USA), donated by Edward D. Libbey, 1926.

134  The *Wartburg* near Eisenach in the Thuringian Forest. Saint Elizabeth lived here in the latter half of the 13th century where also the "Bards' Contest" is supposed to have taken place in the latter half of the 13th century. In the winter of 1521/22 Martin Luther sought refuge here and worked on his Bible translation.

135  *Christian von Brunswick-Wolfenbüttel* (1599–1626) was one of the Conquistadores who crossed Germany and laid waste with their mercenary troops in the Thirty Years' War. This engraving (about 1622) shows the Protestant army commander surrounded by the towns captured by him in Hesse and Westphalia.

136  *Staircase well in Brühl Castle near Cologne*, built between 1740–48 according to plans by Balthasar Neumann. The ceiling fresco is by Carlo Carlone. In the centre of the display wall can be seen the busts of Elector and Archbishop Clemens August.

137  *View of the castle and city of Karlsruhe*. Engraving by Ch. Thran. Together with Mannheim, Karlsruhe is a splendid example of a princely residence during the age of absolutism; from the castle tower all radially-laid streets can be surveyed. The city was founded "as a triumph of rationalism" in 1715 and the grand-ducal castle altered in 1750.

138  *The Margrave's Opera House, Bayreuth*, built between 1744–1748, is an outstanding example of south German Rococo. The residence of the Margraves of Brandenburg-Kulmbach became Bavarian in 1810. Richard Wagner continued the theatre tradition of Bayreuth through the construction of the Festival House between 1872–1876.

139  *Garden figure in Veitshöchheim*. The summer palace of the prince-bishops of Würzburg became famous because of its park with the numerous statues by Ferdinand Dietz.

140  *Wall pavilion of the Zwinger, Dresden*, built in 1711–22 by Daniel Pöppelmann (1662–1736) for court festivities. The statue decoration by Balthasar Permoser (1651–1732) is a fine example of German Baroque.

141  *Heinrich, Baron of Gagern* (1799–1880), was elected president of the Frankfurt National Assembly. He ranks among the champions of parliamentary democracy in Germany.

142  *Karl, Imperial Baron vom und zum Stein* (1757–1831), the great reformer of Prussia, was an enemy of absolutism and supported the idea of German unity. His name will forever be linked with the emancipation of the peasants, municipal autonomy and the creation of modern forms of state administration.

143  *Wilhelm Emanuel, Baron von Ketteler* (1811–1877), bishop of Mainz, was one of the leading Catholic church leaders of his time. As a deputy in the National Assembly 1848/49 and the Imperial Parliament 1871/72 he stood out for alleviation of social distress through laws and self-help facilities for the working classes.

144  *Claus, Count Schenk von Stauffenberg* (1907–1944), a leading member of the resistance movement against the Nazi regime, took it upon himself to smuggle a bomb into Hitler's HQ. Following the failure of the plot, Stauffenberg was executed in the yard of the Bendlerstrasse, Berlin, on the 20th July 1944.

145  *Thurn and Taxis postage-stamps* from the Franz Hottenroth Collection, Munich.

146  *Thurn and Taxis carriage museum in Regensburg*. The princes of Thurn and Taxis, as "Postmasters General" in the German Empire and the Netherlands, laid the foundations of the modern postal system.

147  *The Porta Nigra in Trier*, originally a gateway in the Roman city fortress (3rd century AD). With its front façade facing east, it is an architectural expression of imperial power.

149  *Osthoven Gate, Soest*, built between 1523–1526. Soest was granted full city status already at the beginning of the 12th century and became subsequently one of the leading Hanseatic cities.

150  *Statue of Roland in front of Bremen town hall:* Symbol of city freedom, erected in 1404, looking towards the cathedral of the bishop who constituted a threat to the citizens' freedom.

151  *Eagle on the market fountain, Goslar*. At the beginning of the 13th century, Emperor Henry III built an extensive palace in Goslar; granted city status in 1110, Goslar became a Free Imperial City in 1340.

152  *Figures of sentinels above the town hall entrance in Regensburg* from 1408. The warrior figures "Schutz and Trutz" symbolize the will of the citizens of the Free Imperial City to assert themselves in the face of any form of force.

153  *The 'Golden Tower' in Regensburg* is the highest of some 50 remaining

house towers of the merchant families (built in the 13th century) which served both as dwelling places and secure warehouses.

154 *Jacob Fugger with his book-keeper, Matthäus Schwartz*. Miniature from the year 1516 now in the Duke Anton Ulrich Museum, Brunswick. Under the direction of Jacob Fugger and his brothers, the Augsburg commercial enterprise became the most powerful banking house in Europe.

155 *Fair-charter granted to the city of Frankfurt*, from the year 1240. Emperor Frederick II grants his protection to visitors to the Frankfurt Fair.

156 *Merchants' Hall in the market place, Freiburg* in the Breisgau, built between 1524–1532. Between the windows are the statues of Maximilian I, Charles V, Ferdinand I and Philip II.

157 *City wall of Rothenburg ob der Tauber*, a gem amongst the medieval cities still intact in Germany.

158 *Patricians' houses, Lübeck*. In the Middle Ages the Hansa city of Lübeck was, apart from Cologne, the largest city in North Germany; it owed its wealth and power to its flourishing maritime trade. Thomas Mann, born in Lübeck, describes the fate of a Lübeck patrician's family in his novel 'Buddenbrooks'.

159 *Self-portrait of Adam Krafft* in the House of Sacraments in the St. Laurence Church, Nuremberg, 1493–1496. The artist represents himself in a very natural way as the head of a craftsmen's community and pronounces thereby the self-confidence of the craftsmen's class.

160 *The "Nuremberg Egg"* of Peter Henlein (Hehle), 1480–1542, who invented the 'balance' to regulate the movement of small watches making possible thereby the construction of pocket watches.

161 *The public weigher relief by Adam Krafft* at St. Sebald's Church, Nuremberg. Exact measures and weights were the basis of regulated trade and business in civic communities, particularly since the guilds imposed strict rules for trading goods for craftmen's products.

162 *Bakers' Guild tankard* from Neisse, about 1490. Height 2ft 4ins, capacity 4 gallons. Engraved with figures of apostles and saints.

163 *Guild panel of the Master Dyers*. Centre piece of the Master's Panel from the year 1685 in the Ulm Museum, portraying the dyers at work and their coat-of-arms.

164 *The Fuggerei (almshouses) in Augsburg*. Jacob Fugger founded a residential settlement consisting of six streets and a chapel for poor and elderly citizens; it is the oldest social settlement in the world. The houses, built by the architect Thomas Krebs between 1516–1523, are inhabited today by old-age pensioners who still only pay a yearly rent fixed at that time i. e. 1 guilder (just over DM 1.25).

165 *The Holy Spirit Old People's Home, Lübeck*. Following the pattern of the Holy Spirit Old People's Home founded in Rome by Pope Innocent III, numerous such establishments for the poor and the old in the cities were donated in the 13th century by rich citizens.

166 *St. Annen's House, Goslar*, a former monastery, was converted in 1494 into a home for elderly ladies as a civic donation.

167 *The Holy Spirit Old People's Home, Nuremberg* endowed in 1331 by the mayor, Konrad Gross, was extended between 1488–1527 by the addition of a sick bay over an arm of the river Pegnitz.

168 *Cologne council meeting at the beginning of the 17th century*, from an engraving by J. Toussyn in the Municipal Museum, Cologne. The representatives of the citizens face each other in the old seating order as equals. The mayor and the treasurer are seated under the cross.

169 *Council meeting in Ulm*. In the council of the former Free Imperial City of Ulm the old circular seating order of equal assignment has been retained to the present day.

170 *Town hall square in Lübeck*. A Free Imperial City since 1226, Lübeck was the most powerful city in the Hanseatic League. Towards the end of the 13th century "Lübeck Law" was valid in over a hundred cities in the Baltic area including Reval and Novgorod. The oldest part of the town hall dates from the 13th century.

171 *Mayor Carl Constanz Victor Fellner* (1807–1866) committed suicide in protest against the loss of Imperial Freedom when Prussian troops occupied the Free Imperial City of Frankfurt in 1866.

172 *Konrad Adenauer* (1870–1967), the first chancellor of the Federal Republic of Germany, gained his political experience as mayor of Cologne from 1917–1933; through a generous town-planning programme he safeguarded Cologne's development and a broad green belt.

173 *Karl Goerdeler* (1884–1945), mayor of Leipzig, was executed in 1945 as one of the leaders of the resistance movement against Hitler.

174 *The town hall in Augsburg*, building of which was started in 1615 by Elias Holl, is one of the most impressive pieces of Renaissance architecture in Germany.

175 *Ernst Reuter* (1889–1953), first Socialist mayor of Berlin, earned great distinction for himself, particularly during the blockade in 1948/49, in his efforts for the city's independence.

176 *Hans-Jochen Vogel*, born 1926. Since 1960 Social Democratic mayor of Munich.

177 *Bensberg town hall* in Rhineland was built between 1964–1967 according to plans by the architect Gottfried Böhm. The intention is to interpret in a modern way the old idea of the 'municipal crown'; further towers can be added as and when required.

178 *City-centre, Munich*. The former Bavarian ducal city is today one of the Federal Republic's economic and cultural centres. In the centre of the photograph is the Church of Our Lady, rebuilding of which began in 1473; top left, the ducal residence, built in the 16th and 17th centuries.

179 *The protest march of the Silesian weavers*. Käthe Kollwitz (1867–1945) made social distress in the industrial age the subject of artistic indictment. The protest march of the Silesian weavers (1844) driven on by hunger and desperation was put down by police and military.

180 *My Father–My Mother* by Otto Dix (1891–1969). Painting in the Lower Saxony State Museum, Hanover. This expressionist painter captured above all in his work, man's experiences of existence in the 20th century, social distress and war.

181 *Mechanical forge near Wegscheid* in the Bavarian Forest. Driven by mill-wheels, mechanical forging recall the early forms of industrialization.

182 *Works shop-floor about 1910*. With increasing industrialization, working man became the slave of machines.

183 *Berlin tenement house about 1900*, in Ackerstrasse. Under the banner of industrialization, the population of Berlin increased enormously from 421,000 in 1852 to 3.2 million by 1905. The street plan of 1858 laid the foundations for the tenement building pattern; up to 325 people could be housed in a six-storey block. Not until the Eighties were living

conditions gradually made more humane. The elimination of degrading living conditions was one of the main political concerns of the Social Democratic Party.

*184 The Ludwigshafen-Edigheim estate* as an example of modern planning; a combination of detached houses and sky-scrapers.

*185 Birthplace of Karl Marx in Trier. – Title page of the first edition*
*186 of the "Manifesto of the Communist Party"* (1818–1883). Born of
*189* Jewish parents in Trier, he joined, together with *Friedrich Engels* (1820–1895), the 'Federation of Communists' in Brussels, for whom he wrote the 'Communist Manifesto'.

*187 Adolf Kolping* (1813–1865), a trained shoemaker and later a Catholic priest, founded local clubs for journey-men in Elberfeld and Cologne, from which developed the Catholic movement of Journeymen's Clubs.

*188 Johann Hinrich Wichern* (1808–1881) was the founder of the Home Mission and the father of the protestant 'Diakonie' (care of the sick). To counter child-distress he set up the social institute "Rough House".

*190 Franz Josef von Buss* (1803–1878) took up the struggle against child-labour. As the leader of southwest German political Catholicism and champion of social reforms, he became the president of the first Catholic convention in 1848. A lithograph by Schertle in the Municipal Archives, Karlsruhe.

*191 May Day poster of 1901 – May Day celebrations 1966 in Berlin.*
*192* Since the resolution of the Second Internationale in 1889, the 1st May has been World Labour Day. In Germany, the May Day celebrations contributed decisively towards making the demands of the workers
*193* known in public. In the Federal Republic, the *Federation of German Trade Unions* (DGB) with its almost 7 million members has been first and foremost in making the working class a factor in modern economic and social policy in the state.

*194 Leaflet commemorating the Congress of Unification of the German*
*195 Social Democrats in Gotha, May 1875. – Statute of the German Workers' Union.* The history of the German workers' movement began in May, 1863, with the founding of the German Workers' Union by Ferdinand Lasalle. In 1869, Wilhelm Liebknecht and August Bebel, both followers of Karl Marx, launched the Social Democratic Workers' Party, standing firmly on the ground of international Socialism. In 1875 the two groups combined in Gotha (Gotha Programme) to become the German Socialist Workers' Party.

*196 Kurt Schuhmacher* (1895–1952), after long years of internment in a concentration camp, became the chairman of the German Social Democratic Party in May, 1946 and party whip for the Social Democrats in the Federal Parliament from 1949 until his death.

*197 Cooperative Society store in Chemnitz.* Following the English pattern, cooperative societies sprang up in Germany as self-help organizations for the working class. Statutory social security took initially the form of insurance likewise based on organised self-help; the first social security laws were created by Otto von Bismarck in the years 1883–1889.

*198 Student hostel of the 'Arbeiterwohlfahrt,' (Welfare Organisation)*, one of the relief organizations, non-denominational and independent of politics, founded in 1919 by Marie Juchacz, Social Democratic member of the Imperial Parliament.

*199 Programme of the premiere of 'The Weavers' in 1893.* Gerhart Haupt-

mann's dramatic portrayal of the Silesian weavers' revolt in 1844 describes their desperate plight. Emperor William II gave up his box at the theatre when this 'Subversive Drama', initially forbidden by the police, was performed in 1894.

*200 Bert Brecht "Puntila and his servant Matti".* Performance by the Munich Kammerspiele in 1964 (premiere 1948 in Zürich). Bert Brecht portrays, via the landowner Puntila and his irreverent servant Matti, the duality and inconsistency of a system of society in need of reform.

*201 "State of emergency or the strolling players are coming".* Performance by the Westphalian State Theatre Castrop-Rauxel, 1968. The writer Max von der Grün (born 1926) worked for years as a miner in the Ruhr; he is co-founder of the Dortmund "Group 61" which is trying to express artistically the world of industrial labour.

*202 Final assembly in the Volkswagen Works – At the assembly line – Regulat-*
*203 ing valves in the Bayer Chemical Works.* A round 8 million people are
*204* employed in industry in the Federal Republic of Germany, a bare third of whom are women. Male workers earn an average weekly wage (1970) of DM 228,–, female about DM 146,–.

*205 The Werner Works* for telephone, telegraph, cable, engineering and data processing of Siemens AG, Munich, Hofmannstrasse.

*206 Inflation bank note.* The inflation of 1923, the result of war expenditure and reparations shattered the economy of the German Empire, destroyed all savings deposits and robbed the people of a financially sound foundation. In order to clear the huge debt of 405,000 million Reichsmarks resulting from the bankrupt estate of Hitler's Reich, a currency reform was introduced in 1948, which devalued the paper money in circulation and which gave impetus to all productive forces. Twice within 25 years the German national wealth in money and securities were devalued to less than a tenth.

*207 Refugees.* In two world wars Germany lost 8.5 million people within one generation. As a result of the war provoked by Hitler, 16 million Germans were expelled from their settlement areas, mainly in Eastern Europe, between 1944 and 1950.

*208 Buried under the rubble* in World War II, in the area of the Federal Republic, were 2.2 million dwellings i.e. a good 20 % of the houses. The result was a fundamental displacement in the sociological structure of the cities; long established burghers' families were frequently replaced by newcomers to the area.

*209 The "Hohe Strasse" in Cologne.* This street, completely destroyed in 1945, and which connects the cathedral district with the New Market, is one of the most impressive shopping centres in the Federal Republic today.

## The idea of the Empire – the empire of ideas

*210 The 'Kaiserberge' in the Hegau area*, Baden-Württemberg.

*211 Charlemagne.* Carved relief on the emperor's shrine in the cathedral treasures, Aachen; goldsmith's work of 1215. Charlemagne bequeathed his palace chapel with numerous reliquaries which made Aachen the most famous place of pilgrimage in Germany.

*212 The Pope and Emperor on a joint throne.* Illustration from the 'Sachsenspiegel' (Code of Old Saxon Laws) portraying the unity of spiritual and secular power in the Holy Roman Empire of the German Nation. The 'Sachsenspiegel' of Eike von Repgow is the oldest German law book, originating from 1220. Manuscript of the Heidelberg University Library, Pal. Germ. 164, about 1300.

213 *Charlemagne's throne in Aachen Cathedral*. The palace chapel was dedicated by Pope Leo III in AD 805. After the assumption of office, the German kings mounted the royal rostrum in the gallery (last occasion 1531), having first been annointed and crowned at the altar. *The emperor as defender of christianity*. Following the victory of Emperor Otto the Great over the Hungarians at the Battle of Lechfeld in AD 955, the most dangerous attack on Western Europe, since the time

215 of the Huns' incursions, was thwarted. *St. Ulrich's Cross* of the Bishop of Augsburg, a product of the late 15th century shows scenes from this battle with the Hungarians. In 1241 a joint Polish-German army stopped the invasion of Mongolian mounted warriors into Western Europe at Liegnitz. From the time the Turks advanced to the gates of Vienna in 1529, the German emperors found themselves involved in permanent defensive warfare for two hundred years; the first great naval victory over the Turkish armada, won by Don John of Austria at the Battle of Lepanto in 1571, was celebrated throughout Germany

214 as an act of salvation. *The Lepanto Monstrance* of Ingolstadt is proof of this. Don John of Austria was born in Regensburg as the natural son

216 of Charles V and Barbara Blomberg. The *Turkish booty* in Baden State Museum, Karlsruhe, bears witness to the eventual victory of the Imperial armies over the Ottoman forces. The chain mail, embellished with gilded silver fastenings and decorative discs, belonged to the supreme commander of the janissaries during the siege of Vienna in 1682. The majority of other items in this collection came from the Battle of Slankamen, north of Belgrade, in which Louis William, Margrave of Baden ("Türkenlouis", 1655–1707), as commander-in-chief of the imperial forces, routed the Turkish army in 1691.

217 *Group of windows in the main hall of the Imperial Castle at Wimpfen*, on the river Neckar, dates from the 13th century and was completed by Emperor Frederick II.

218 *The emperor's living room in Nuremberg Castle*. The castle, built by Emperor Henry III about 1040, was extended in the 13th and 14th centuries. The living rooms of the emperor date from 1487. From the former imperial fortress and the surrounding city assigned to its charge grew, in the course of time, one of the most powerful and art-filled Free Imperial Cities.

219 *The Imperial Cathedral in Worms*. The former Roman city of Civitas Vangionum was the centre of the Burgundian Empire since 413. This favourite residence of the Carolingian dynasty and consequently the scene of numerous imperial and royal gatherings, Worms was given its charter of civic independence in 1184 by Emperor Frederick I. The building of the cathedral was started about AD 1000 and dedicated in 1018. The west choir was built between 1210–1230. At the Imperial Diet of Worms in 1521, Martin Luther professed his teachings in the presence of Emperor Charles V.

220 *Charles V*. Portrait by Titian (1548) in the 'Alte Pinakothek' in Munich. As King of Spain, Charles V (1500–1558), who was elected German king in 1519, ruled over an empire "on which the sun never set."

Crowned emperor in 1530, he tried, in vain, to oppose the spread of Protestantism. Continual armed conflict with France and the Turks forced him to yield to the pressure of the German princes and to agree to the Peace of Augsburg in 1555.

221 *Germany after the Peace of Westphalia 1648*. The feudal princes took advantage of the Thirty Years' War, which resulted from religious dissension, to weaken central imperial authority. The Netherlands and Switzerland left the empire which now consisted of over 300 states or territorial units (princedoms, dukedoms, Imperial cities, bishoprics, abbeys, etc.). The unifying body from 1663 to 1806 was the "Continual Imperial Diet" established permanently in Regensburg (Reproduction from Droyen's 'Hand atlas of World History', 1886; section of the map of Germany in the 17th century).

222 *The Hall of the Imperial Diet in the town hall, Regensburg*, was erected as the council chamber for the city fathers in 1356 and used from 1663 until the decline of the empire for assemblies of the 'Continual Imperial Diet'. The emperor or his representative sat under the canopy, next to him along the wall, the electors, on the right the clergy and on the left the secular princes. The benches in the foreground were reserved for the Free Imperial Cities.

223 *Empress Maria Theresia* (1717–1780) succeeded in consolidating Austrian inherited territories by reforms in administration, trade, and finance.

224 *Frederick II, the Great, of Prussia* (1712–1786)' made Prussia the major power in Germany by a series of successful campaigns. As the representative of enlightened despotism and champion of religious tolerance, as a promoter of trade and industry, he created a state with a modern stamp.

225 *The imperial court room in the prince-bishop's residence, Würzburg*. Built between 1740 and 1745 by Balthasar Neumann and decorated with frescoes by G. B. Tiepolo, the imperial court room displays the ideal unity between the catholic provinces of Germany and the House of Hapsburg.

226 *Charlottenburg Palace, Berlin*, was built during the reign of Elector Frederick III (commenced 1695) who, with the agreement of Leopold I, elevated himself to 'King in Prussia' in Königsberg in 1701.

227 *Andreas Schlüter*, equestrian statue of Elector Frederick William of Brandenburg. The 'Great Elector' (1640–1688) laid the foundations for the rise of Prussia by means of reforms and ambitious building programme. He opened up his land to immigrants – expelled Jews, Waldensians and Huguenots – who at one time comprised a third of Berlin's population.

228 *Crown princess Louisa of Prussia*. The life-size twin statues of the Prussian princesses Louisa, wife of Frederick William III of Prussia (1770–1840) and her sister Frederica, are by the classical sculptor Johann Gottfried Schadow and dates from 1795.

229 A scene from the play "*Prince Frederick of Homburg*" by Heinrich von Kleist (1777–1811) in the Spielhaus, Stuttgart, 1966. The theme of this 'drama of fulfilment of duty' deals with the prince's mental conflict between duty and personal responsibility.

230 *Statue commemorating the Battle of Leipzig* (1813) recalls the victory over Napoleon of the allies Prussia, Austria and Russia under the command of Count Schwarzenberg on the 18th September 1813.

231 *Barricade-fighting in Berlin* on the night of the 18th/19th March 1848. Dreams of democratic freedom and national unity, which had remained unfulfilled since the end of the Napoleonic Wars, led, under the influence of the French February Revolution, to uprisings throughout Germany. The victory of the revolution in Berlin caused the German princes to yield to the demands for the establishment of a national assembly. (Lithograph in the Art Library of the Foundation for Prussian Culture, Berlin).

232 *Count Otto von Bismarck* (1815–1898) solved the German problem according to Prussian ideas by defeating Austria in 1866 which led to the Hapsburg monarchy leaving the German Federation. The Franco-Prussian War (1870–71) assured Prussia's position of political supremacy. William I of Prussia was proclaimed German Emperor in Versailles in 1871. Bismarck's policy was subsequently bent on securing peace in Europe: his domestic policy attempted to achieve a strengthening of conservative forces and at the same time to establish a pattern of society guided by the state (rather than by political parties and the churches).

233 *The National Assembly in St. Paul's Church.* On the 18th May, 1848, the first parliament, the German National Assembly, consisting of representatives of the people, convened in St. Paul's Church, Frankfurt, and by the end of the same year passed the "Law concerning the basic rights of the people". When the Prussian king refused the proffered imperial crown, however, and dissolved the constituent assembly for Prussia, the other princes suppressed the democratic elements likewise. The 'Rump Parliament' which had withdrawn from Frankfurt to Stuttgart was dissolved by the military. As a result, those countless patriots who did not emigrate were imprisoned.

234 *Hermann's statue in the Teutoburg Forest near Detmold*, 1838/75. 86 feet high copper statue of the prince of the Cheruscans, a Teutonic tribe, who annihilated the Roman army of the governor Varus. This is one of the early gigantic statues by which growing nationalism confirmed its conscious feeling of national greatness.

235 *On the 9th November, 1918, Philipp Scheidemann proclaimed the Republic of Germany in Berlin.* The Treaty of Versailles, prohibitively high reparation payments, the occupation of the Ruhr by France and the inflation of 1923 plunged the Weimar Republic into one crisis after another and made it the plaything of extremist parties. The world economic crisis in 1929/32 led to a hitherto unknown mass unemployment and to the radicalization of the struggle between communists and Hitler's followers. The return of Germany to the Community of Nations (1922 Treaty of Rapallo, 1925 Treaty of Locarno, 1926 acceptance into the League of Nations) was unable to prevent the weakening of the republic. With the appointment of Adolf Hitler to Chancellor on the 30th January, 1933, the achievements of Ebert, Stresemann and

236 Brüning were nullified. *The Reichstag fire* on the 27th February, 1933, gave Hitler the perfect excuse to eliminate all democratic elements.

237 *Josef Thorak's studio.* False greatness by a pointless increase in dimensions was typical of many of the statues on Hitler's monstrous party buildings.

238 *Party Rally in Nuremberg, 1935.* The party rallies were the acme of demagogical influence of the masses. And so to mislead world opinion in September 1939, the 'Party Rally of Peace' was held.

239 Inset: *Memorial for the victims of National Socialist rule in Dachau concentration camp* by the Yugoslav sculptor Nadan.

240 The photograph of *Anne Frank* (born 1929 in Frankfurt, died 1945 in Bergen-Belsen concentration camp) whose diary describes the distress

241 of the Jews; *Children in uniform being taken prisoner by American troops* in April 1945.

242 *Corpus Christi procession in Cologne, 1946.* Cologne's catholics walked in the first Corpus Christi procession after the war through a dead and deserted city, 80% of which consisted of rubble.

243 *Trans-Europe Express.* On the 2nd June, 1957, the German Federal Railways put into service the first 10 TEE trains following an international agreement.

244 *Meeting of the Council of Europe in Strasbourg.* The Federal Republic is a member of the Council of Europe, founded in 1949, since 1951.

245 *Robert Schuman*, French Foreign Minister, *Alcide de Gasperi* and *Konrad Adenauer*, first chancellor of the Federal Republic of Germany championed the movement for a United Europe.

246 *Paul-Henri Spaak*, Belgian Foreign Minister and *Walter Hallstein*
247 pleaded for European economic integration. Spaak was one of the initiators of the Montan Union, the European coal and steel community. In 1958, following the setting-up of the European Economic Community, Walter Hallstein assumed office of president of the Common Market.

248 *"Communal Citizens' Oath, Oath of the city of Bremen"*. The swearing
249 of the civic oath from the *'Laienspiegel'* in Worms. The prerequisite for freedom from the yoke of the city feudal lords was the consolidation of the citizens into self-protecting communities. Reciprocal help and voluntary adherence to the resolutions passed by the council elected by the burghers were solemnly sworn. The foundations of civic freedom in many German cities are, therefore, to be found in the citizens' communities and leagues bound by oath (in Cologne 1112). The tradition of the civic oath is still observed today, for example, in the 'Schwörtag' (Oath Day) in Ulm. The original "Communal Citizens' Oath of the City of Bremen" comes from the Vellguth collection, Bonn: Woodcut from the 'Laienspiegel' by Ulrich Tengler, Worms manuscript of 1507.

250 *'Unity, Right and Freedom'*, first line of the third verse of the 'Song of the Germans' from the original manuscript of the poet Hoffmann von Fallersleben, Summer 1841. The 'Deutschlandlied' was declared as the national anthem by the Weimar Republic in 1920; in 1952 the third verse was reintroduced as the national anthem.

251 At the *Hambach Festival* in 1832 the 'United Free States of Germany' and 'a Confederate Republic of Germany' were demanded. The desire for national unity, awakened during the Wars of Liberation against Napoleon, were suppressed by the princes. When revolution broke out in 1830 in Paris, which sparked off uprisings in Belgium, Switzerland, Greece and Poland, there followed similar rebellion in Germany, particularly in Brunswick and Saxony. On the 27th May, 1832, 20,000 people assembled near the ruins of Hambach Castle near Neustadt in the Haardt mountains.

252 *Ferdinand Hodler* (1853–1918) *'Of One Accord'* Painting of a scene from the time of the Reformation in the Hanover town hall, 1913.

253 *The Lüneberg town hall* with court of justice (right), decorated in 1519. Originally most judicial courts were held in open halls in front of the

town hall, later inside. Complete jurisdiction implied sovereignty and laid the foundations of political independence.

254 *The market cross in Trier* is one of the oldest 'monuments of justice' in Germany and proclaims the right to hold a market. It was erected by Archbishop Henry in 958.

255 *Theodor Heuss* (1884-1903), the first Federal President, swearing the oath in September 1949 on the Basic Law of the Federal Republic of Germany.

256 *Scene from the 'Sachsenspiegel'* (see Plate 212). "When the king enters the land, all prisoners will, by law, be at his disposal; and they will be brought before him and taken to his courts or, as a result of the court findings, be released". The king's messenger is standing on the left in front of the castle, to demand the prisoners held in custody there. On the right, another prisoner with the person who apprehended him in the presence of the king as supreme court of authority. Manuscript in Heidelberg University Library, Pal. Germ. 164, about 1300.

257 *Chair of the High Court of Justice, Rottweil*, second half of the 18th century. The High Court of Justice, mentioned as early as 1299 and directly responsible to the emperor, convened in the 'open royal street' and was empowered to decide law cases from other judicial districts; thus everyone had the right to appeal directly to the emperor.

258 *Freedom Banner of the Peasants' Revolt*. Woodcut of 1524. The growing despotism of the secular and ecclesiastical overlords drove the people into revolt; the ideas on reform which aimed at a strengthening of central imperial power were given no support, however, by Emperor Charles V, who was a stranger in the land.

259 *Civil liberties of the burghers of Mainz* from the year 1181, engraved in the bronze rings of the market portal of Mainz Cathedral, were to remind the city lords of the citizens' rights.

260 *Title page of the first impression of Martin Luther's pamphlet entitled "Concerning the freedom of a Christian"* (1520). Gospel and belief are portrayed as the only pillar for Christians; in spiritual matters man is free and subject to no one.

261 *Disputation*, engraving by Hans Burgkmair. The disputation as a means of forming opinions or explaining scientific problems had flourished during the Reformation. The best known was the Leipzig Disputation of 1519, which Luther led with Eck and Karlstadt, on the question of predestination and the authority of the Pope and councils.

262 *"The Hessian Messenger"*, 1834. The Socialist pamphlet by the young Büchner (1813-1837) called for the struggle ("Peace to the huts, war to the palaces") against political suppression and social grievances in his Hessian homeland. See Plate 277.

263 *"The Robbers"*. Performance by the Residenztheater in Munich, 1968. "In tyrannos" was the motto of Friedrich Schiller's (1759-1805) first play "The Robbers". Premiere in Mannheim, 1782. His tempestuous call for freedom made it the most significant drama of the 'Storm and Stress' era. See Plate 276.

264 *Albrecht Dürer, The Four Riders of the Apocalypse*. Dürer (1471-1528), together with Mathias Grünewald (ca. 1460/70-1528) and Albrecht Altdorfer (1480-1538), is amongst the leading German artists of the transition period from the Middle Ages to modern times. In numerous woodcuts and engravings he transferred the Bible story into a world as imagined by people at that time.

265 *Wolf Huber, Bridge in the Mountains*. Huber (ca. 1485-1553) is, together with Altdorfer, the leading master of the 'Danube school'. The new visual appreciation of that time for the reality of nature finds its expression predominantly in his landscapes with their accurate and detailed realism.

266 *Albrecht Altdorfer, The Battle of Issus*. This painting (1528) of Alexander's victory over the Persian king Darius at Issus portrays this historical incident as a strange happening, since the atmosphere and the stars seem to be involved. By a rounding of the horizon the spherical shape of the world is suggested–the first time that the reality of the world was captured artistically. This famous painting, now in the Alte Pinakothek, Munich, accompanied Napoleon on his campaigns. Altdorfer (1480-1538) carried out his work in Regensburg, his final position being that of municipal architect.

267 *Wilhelm von Hirsau's astrolabe*, ca. 1060, Municipal Museum, Regensburg. On the capital of a pillar kneels Aratus, a famous author of astronomical interpretations in the Middle Ages. "The movement of the stars followed by Aratus's rod". On the reverse side of the disc is a projection of the heavens' orbits. The astrolabe was used for observing the stars and their position.

268 *Room in Kepler's house, Regensburg*. Johannes Kepler (1571-1630), one of the main founders of modern astronomy, was the first to give a dynamic explanation of the planets' movements; he was of the belief that the movements of the planets were caused by a force emanating from the sun.

269 *Johannes Gutenberg's printing press* in the Gutenberg Museum, Mainz. Johannes Gensfleisch (1400-1468) became the inventor of printing by the use of moveable type.

270 *Gottfried Wilhelm Leibniz* (1646-1716), philosopher, physicist, historian and politician, was the greatest scholar of rationalism. Thus he developed, independent of Newton, infinitesimal calculus and was amongst the first to recognise the validity of the principle of the conservation of energy. As a philosopher he outlined a pattern of rationalistic-idealistic ideas which sought to reconcile the mechanistic explanation of natural phenomena with religious belief.

271 *Guericke's experiment with the Magdeburg hemispheres*. By pumping two hollow hemispheres empty, Otto von Guericke (1662-1686) proved the substance of air; he constructed the first water barometer and invented the friction electricity machine.

272 *Johann Sebastian Bach* (1685-1750) is, together with Handel, the main representative of Baroque music. His works are the synthesis of a century-long development in music. Main works: "The well-tempered clavicord", "The Art of the Fugue", Passions, "Mass in B-Minor".

273 *Immanuel Kant* (1724-1804) introduced a turning point in the history of western philosophy in his "Criticism of Pure Reason" which examines the limits of man's perception; his ideas signify the conclusion and overcoming of the Age of Reason as well as the point of departure for new philosophic paths (German Idealism, New Kantalism, Positivism, etc.).

274 *Johann Wolfgang von Goethe* (born 1749 in Frankfurt-on-Main, died 1832 in Weimar), greatest German poet, besides being a physicist and statesman, became known through his simple and hymnic lyric poetry

and achieved world fame by his passionate novel in epistolary form "The Sufferings of the Young Werther" (1774). In stage plays such as "Clavigo", "Stella", "Urfaust" (concerned with the problem of genius) and "Götz von Berlichingen" Goethe raises the fundamental questions of freedom and humanity (Egmont, Iphigenia, Tasso). From 1794 onwards, Goethe worked in close cooperation with Friedrich Schiller, became manager-director of the court theatre in Weimar and simultaneously carried out scientific research (theory of colours). 1795/96 "Wilhelm Meister's Apprenticeship" and 1797 the epic "Hermann and Dorothea". In his old age, a wise belief in life and a harmonious view of the world. To the last engaged in his autobiography "Poetry and Truth", "The Journeyman's Travels" and Part 2 of "Faust".

275 *Georg Wilhelm Friedrich Hegel* (1770–1831). Portrait by Jack Schlesinger. Hegel, as a perfectionist of German idealism, created one of the greatest speculative systems in the history of European philosophy. He sought to understand 'universal rationalism' in natural phenomena and in history. The 'mind' is, for him, the truth of all reality. His philosophy is a systematic processing of intellectual substance in history. Hegel's theories on state, law and society exercised great influence; he also directly affected Karl Marx, and in our time Jean-Paul Sartre, inducing thereby two very different trains of philosophy in the present century.

276 *Friedrich Schiller*, portrait by G. von Kügelgen. Schiller's (1759–1805) literary efforts and theoretical writing played a decisive role in the classical era, always taking the idea of freedom as the central theme. This demand that the theatre should be a 'moral institute' made a fundamental contribution to the establishment of the middle-class national theatre. In later years, he enjoyed close friendship with Goethe.

277 *Georg Büchner* (1813–1837). With stark realism and passionate language, Büchner ("Danton's Death") depicts the destruction of the individual through the "terrible fatalism of history" and ("Woyzeck") man as the helpless victim of his environment and society.

278 *Heinrich Heine* (1797–1856). Etching by L. F. Grimm. Heine was not only an outstanding lyric poet but also the creator of the modern feuilleton. He polemized against the restoration and had to go into exile to Paris in 1831. His poems, set to music by Schubert and Schumann have, in many cases, become folk-songs (e.g. Loreley).

279 *Schiller's birthplace in Marbach-on-Neckar*. Nowadays, the Schiller National Museum and the German Literature Archives are situated in Marbach.

280 *Johann Gottlieb Fichte* (1762–1814) was, together with Schelling and Hegel, one of the champions of German idealism. His 'scientific teaching' was based on the 'dialectic method' which achieved universal historic fame through Hegel and Marx. His "Addresses to the German nation" encouraged the uprising against Napoleon's occupation of Germany.

281 *Alexander von Humboldt* (1769–1859). Portrait by Kaspar Stieler in the Art Gallery, Potsdam. Because of his comprehensive knowledge, Humboldt ranks among the universal scholars of the Western World. His expeditions to America and Asia in his capacity as natural scientist and geographer gained him the friendship of outstanding scholars and statesmen in both the Old and the New World.

282 *Ludwig van Beethoven* (1770–1827). Portrait by G. Waldmüller. Resi-

dent in Vienna from 1792 onwards, he forms, together with Haydn and Mozart, the triumvirate of the Viennese Classicists. Beethoven is the first great free-lance musician. Many of his musical themes were interpreted as ideas. The central point of his creative activity, representing the completion and rebirth of an era at one and the same time, comprises piano concertos, symphonies and string quartetts.

283 *Beethoven's birthplace*. The composer was born in the back part of this modest Rococo house in the Bonngasse, Bonn, on 17th December, 1770. Nowadays, it is a museum and the adjoining building houses the Beethoven Archives.

284 *Caspar David Friedrich* (1774–1840) '*Two men contemplating the moon*'. 1889. C. D. Friedrich's works are strongly influenced by romantic melancholy and devout religious belief. In his landscapes, man is often portrayed as a creature lost in his environment or the universe.

285 *Jacob* (1785–1863) *and Wilhelm* (1786–1859) *Grimm* are still best known today for collecting, revising and editing "children's fairy stories". Founders of the scientific research into German folklore, language, literature, mythology and law: "German Dictionary'.

286 *Joseph, Baron von Eichendorff* (1788–1857), portrait by J. Rabe. Eichendorff was the most popular poet of the German Romantic Movement. Robert Schumann and Hugo Wolf set many of his poems to music.

287 *Neuschwanstein Castle* near Füssen in the Allgäu, built according to plans made by the theatrical decorator Jank von Dollmann between 1869 and 1886 in neo-Romantic style for King Louis II of Bavaria.

288 *Carl Spitzweg, The Stork is coming*. The Munich artist (1808–1885), with his endearing and whimsical motives, belongs to the late Romantic era.

289 *Robert Schumann* (1810–1856). Chief representative of the Romantic Movement in music and founder of the 'Neue Zeitschrift für Musik'; piano works and songs.

290 *An evening with Ludwig Tieck*. Drawing by L. Pietsch in the Austrian National Library, Vienna. As one of the early Romantic poets and translators (of Shakespeare), Tieck (1773–1853) offered, above all, inspiration to others.

291 *Carl Maria von Weber* (1786–1826). Portrait by C. Jäger. With his opera 'Der Freischütz', Weber, who was a pupil of Michael Haydn, founded the German Romantic Opera.

292 *Felix Mendelssohn-Bartholdy* (1809–1847), the leading composer of the Classical Movement in music, he exercised, by his melody-structure and wealth of form, a great influence on 19th century music.

293 *Johannes Brahms* (1833–1897), as a composer of the late Romantic Movement, combined artistic and human contrasts. His sweeping melodies and austere harmonies contrast sharply with the intensity of feeling in his songs.

294 *Tristan and Isolde*, opera by Richard Wagner (1813–1883), premiere 1865. A performance of the Bayreuth Festival under the direction of Wieland Wagner. The Romantic Movement in music reached its climax with Richard Wagner. His ideas on infinite melody, leitmotif, a musically comprehensive work of art and new harmonies with rich chromatic forms had a fundamental effect on musical development from Anton Bruckner to Arnold Schönberg.

295 *Karl Marx*. See Plates 185 and 186.

296  *Rudolf Diesel* (1858–1913) developed (up to 1897) the diesel engine in cooperation with the Augsburg Machine Works and the firm of Krupp, Essen.

297  *Paul Ehrlich* (1854–1915). An associate of Robert Koch at the Berlin Institute for Infectious Diseases, 1899, director of the Institute for Experimental Therapy in Frankfurt-on-Main. He laid the scientific foundations for the production of high quality antitoxic serums and is regarded as one of the creators of modern chemotherapy.

298  *Daimler motor-car*. Gottlieb Daimler (1834–1900) developed the gas engine together with Nikolaus Otto (1832–1891) and built the first light internal combustion engine in 1883. In 1886 he constructed the first useable motor-car.

299  *Johann Philipp Reis* (1834–1874) is regarded as the inventor of the telephone: his model, which he presented to the 'Physics Association' in Frankfurt in 1861, was further developed by Alexander Graham Bell.

300  *Robert Koch* (1843–1910) laid important foundations of method procedure in bacteriological research and proved conclusively for the first time that the anthrax germ was a living micro-organism and was the cause of an infectious disease. Research expeditions to India and Africa. He found the cholera virus and received the Nobel Prize for Medicine in 1905, for his discoveries in the field of tuberculosis.

301  *Albert Einstein* (1879–1955). By his Special and General Theories of Relativity in 1905 und 1916, provided completely new bases for modern physics. In recognition of his services in theoretical physics, he received the Nobel Prize in 1921.

302  *Wilhelm Conrad Röntgen* (1845–1923) discovered the X-ray (1895) and was given the first Nobel Prize for Physics in 1901.

303  *Werner von Siemens* (1816–1892) invented the electrical dial telegraph and gutta-percha insulation of electric cables, the double T anchor; the Telegraph Construction Company which he founded with J. G. Halske, laid the great underground telegraph line from Berlin to Frankfurt in 1848–49. In 1879, the first electric locomotives and the first electric loom were constructed.

304  *Ferdinand, Count von Zeppelin* (1838–1917). Inventor and constructor of rigid airships.

305  *Berthold Brecht* (1898–1956) gave new practical and theoretical impulses to the theatre, in which he portrays social conditions robbed of illusion and attacks the bourgeoisie on the stage. He emigrated in 1933 and from 1945 onwards was a theatre director in East Berlin.

306  *Thomas Mann* (1875–1955), novelist and essayist; received the Nobel Prize for Literature in 1929 for his novel "Die Buddenbrooks".

307  *Paul Klee* (1879–1940), painter and graphical artist of Swiss origin lived and worked in Germany for the most part, inter alia, as a teacher at the Bauhaus.

308  *Paul Hindemith* (1895–1963). A leading composer of "new music" and finally of the neo-Romantic Movement. Best known opera: "Matthis, the painter". Chamber music, orchestral music, songs.

309  *With the film "Blue Angel"* (1929) based on the novel "Professor Unrat" by Heinrich Mann (1871–1950), Marlene Dietrich achieved world fame. In this UFA film, Emil Jannings played the part of the grammar school professor Unrat.

310  *The Bauhaus*. The haute école of architecture and form was founded in 1919 by Walter Gropius in Weimar and was transferred to Dessau in 1925. Artists associated with the Bauhaus (Kandinsky, Klee, Feininger and Schlemmer) strove to make expediency a guiding principle of form. Banned in 1933, the Bauhaus recommenced its activities as the new Bauhaus in 1937 in Chicago.

311  *Walter Gropius* (1883–1969), founder and constructor of the Bauhaus gave trail-blazing impulses through his "new objectivity in architectural design" (industry and housing).

312  *Meeting of Nobel Prizewinners in Lindau 1965*. On the initiative of Count Bernadotte, Nobel Prizewinners from Germany and other countries meet annually for an exchange of ideas at Lindau on Lake Constance. Front row (from left to right): Rudolf Mössbauer (Nobel Prize for Physics 1961), Richard Kuhn (Chemistry Prize 1938), Werner Heisenberg (Physics Prize 1932), Otto Hahn (Chemistry Prize 1944), Max Born (Physics Prize 1954), Gustav Hertz (Physics Prize 1925) and in front of the microphone, Werner Forssmann (Medicine Prize 1956).

## Germany today

When the Basic Law of the Federal Republic of Germany came into force on the 23rd May, 1949, it was uncertain whether the western part of Germany, completely disorganised both economically and socially by World War II and its after-effects, would be equal to the high demands of the new constitution. With the Basic Law, which in Article 20 established the Federal Republic as a democratic and socially constitutional state, an attempt was made, in a part of the former German Reich, to revive the young democratic tradition of the Weimar Republic. Today it can no longer be doubted that the democratic form of this country is borne by all classes and sectors of society. The partici-

313  pation in the elections for the *Federal German Parliament (Bundestag)*, the heart of legislative power in parliamentary democracy, may be regarded as proof of this: whereas in 1949 21% of the electorate did not make use of their votes, participation in the federal elections in 1953 rose to 86% and in 1965 to 87%. In order to prevent an endangering of the work in parliament through numerous political splinters group, as in the Weimar Republic, the Basic Law denies entry into parliament to those parties gaining less than 5% of the vote.

The parties represented in parliament indicate that the political views of the electorate are governed pragmatically rather than ideologically. Although ten political parties were represented in parliament in 1949, the political mandate of the electorate concentrated more and more on the three major parties, i.e. the Christian Democratic/Christian Socialist Union (CDU/CSU), the German Social Democratic Party (SPD) and the Free Democratic Party (FDP), which with different coalitions have formed the various governments.

326  From 1949–1965 the chairman of the CDU, *Konrad Adenauer – 328, 444* – one of the most outstanding personalities of post-war politics, held the post of federal chancellor. He was followed in 1966 by the

327  father of the "Economic Miracle", *Ludwig Erhard* (CDU), who formed a coalition government with the FDP after the elections in 1965.

329  The Grand Coalition between CDU/CSU and SPD under *Kurt Georg*

Kiesinger – 339, 448, 449 – was replaced by the first SPD/FDP coalition
330 of the Federal Republic under *Willy Brandt* – 347, 348, 447, 450 – and
349 Foreign Minister *Walter Scheel.*

Thanks mainly to the respect which the highest representatives of the
321 state, Federal President *Theodor Heuss* (1949–1959) died 1963, *Hein-*
322 *rich Lübke* (1959–1969) and 323,331 *Gustav Heinemann* (since 1969),
and other statesmen such as Adenauer and Brandt, earned themselves,
the young republic succeeded in establishing its international position.
451–452 The integration of the Federal Republic in the *North Atlantic
Treaty Organization* (NATO) in 1954, the renunciation of national
325 armed forces, the setting up of the *Organization for European Economic*
326 *Cooperation* in 1957 and the *reconciliation with France* were major
contributory factors in the overcoming of mistrust towards the newly-
developing German state. Foreign policy, in view of the East-West
confrontation, sought close association with the western defence sys-
328 tem. *Contact with the Russian leaders,* which led to the release of the
last POW's and the establishment of diplomatic relations between the
Federal Republic and the USSR, caused a sensation. A second German
state was set up on the territory of the Soviet Zone of Occupation,
495–502 thereby isolating *West Berlin* geographically; the capital of the
516 former German Reich, *industrial metropolis* of Europe, 506–515 *intellectual and cultural centre* of Germany, linked firmly with the Federal
Republic in spite of its insular situation, became the symbol of the
505 division of Germany before the erection of the *Wall* in 1961 and the
320 closing off of the *Brandenburg Gate,* so rich in tradition.

If at that time the Federal Republic's foreign policy was dictated by
the basic requirements of security, the government, today, is trying to
449 establish normal *relations with Eastern Europe,* particularly with the
450 *USSR,* in an era of relaxation of tension, and decisive social and
332–337 political changes. *Integration in the cultural sphere* will find its
338 climax in *Munich* in 1972 at the Olympic Games, which will not be
merely a sports event.

The reorientation is not restricted, however, merely to the Federal
Republic's international relations. After years of economic development, an ever-increasing consciousness of the democratisation of
society in all walks of life can be strongly felt. As a sign of the modern
productive society, the mergence of town and country areas by modern
401–407 communications and *rationalization of agricultural production
methods* is being realised.

352 In place of mistrust of the removal of authoritarian power structures
in state and economy, first demanded by 353, 386 *intellectuals* and
leftist radical *student groups,* has come the realisation that the un-
democratic remains of the last century can be replaced only by active
377 cooperation and joint-responsibility in all socially relevant decision proc-
380 esses: *School children and students* are working as equal partners in the
re-shaping of *schools* and *universities, Trade Unions* are demanding an
412 extension of management-employee co-determination 384, 390 *clergy
and laymen* are questioning the tradition-bound authority of the church.
The success of the initiative directed at democratisation will depend
largely on the measure of success in making available specialized knowledge and sources of information to classes of society other than the
traditionally privileged. Co-determination requires that an efficient
362–384 *education system* should not only professionally qualify the indi-

vidual according to ability and aptitude, but should also teach citizens
to be conscious of their responsibilities and critical in a democratic
society. For the marked economic up-swing in the Federal Republic
427–441 not only makes possible increased *prosperity* and shorter working
hours but also brings in its wake, unless people are educated towards
joint-responsibility and towards a conscious shaping of all walks of life,
the danger of an uncritical and prosperous society based primarily on
levels of achievement. The shortening of working hours through progressive industrialization and rationalization of working processes have
allowed people to enjoy an ever increasing proportion of free-time.
427–428 *Travel, festivals* and 437–441 *hobbies* are removing old prejudices
in ever increasing measure.
336–337 *Sport* enjoys a particularly prominent role: the achievements of
German players in foreign teams and vice-versa transcend linguistic
and geographical boundaries.

A faithful reflection of social questions may be found in the cultural
462 sphere. Authors, lyric poets and essayists such as *Erich Kästner,*
515 *Walter Höllerer,* 463 *Hans Magnus Enzensberger* and 466 *Jürgen Becker,*
465 the short story writer *Gabriele Wohmann,* novelists and playwrights
353 such as *Günter Grass,* author of "The Tin Drum", 461 *Martin Walser*
464 and *Heinrich Böll,* author of "The Clown", the novels on divided
459 Germany by *Uwe Johnson* and the literary meetings of the authors'
"Group 47" are known far beyond the German borders.

The international character of book production is presented annually
at the "Frankfurt Book Fair" with its world-wide associations. The
"Peace Prize" of the German Book Industry, which is presented
annually at the Fair, has been received by writers such as the lyric poet
332 *Nelly Sachs,* the politicians 457 *Sarvepalli Rhadakrishnan* and Theo-
379 dor Heuss and the sociologist *Alexander Mitscherlich.*
473–476 The theatre and 460 cabaret, a both representative and topical
forum, presents German and foreign authors, actors and singers. The
513 chanson-singer *Hildegard Knef,* the East Berlin Brecht-Ensemble under
514 the directorship of *Helene Weigel,* actors such as 499 *Martin Held,*
506 directors such as *Fritz Kortner,* 509 *Erwin Piscator,* and 476 *Peter Stein,*
335 guest performances by *Gustav Gründgens* in Moscow and New York,
473 the play 'Marat' by *Peter Weiss,* 474 Peter Handke's 'Kaspar' and the
production by Tankred Dorst's "Toller" has internationally established the German Theatre once more. Some 250 theatres are subsi-
477 dized and even smaller towns can boast of a *modern* new *theatre.*
478 German and non-German composers and conductors such as *Igor
480 Stravinsky, Hans Rosbaud* and *Pierre Boulez* or 479 *Karlheinz Stockhausen* take the stage at International Festivals in Donaueschingen and
Darmstadt, where young composers and new contemporary musical
compositions from many lands provide a basis for lively discussion.
A meeting-point for famous conductors such as Herbert von Karajan
481 and Leonard Bernstein is provided by the *Berlin Philharmonic* built
508 by *Hans Scharoun.*
484 In music and the *music theatre,* the great tradition in these fields lives
469 on through the works of *Carl Orff,* 469 *Werner Egk,* 471 *Hans Werner
470 Henze, Bernd Alois Zimmermann,* 468 *Wilhelm Killmayer,* 472 *Nicolaus
A. Huber,* with annual first performances and by commissioning na-
484 tional, non-German composers and directors such as *Günter Rennert*
485 and *Vaclav Kaslik.*

*482–485* For the first time since the end of World War II, an independent *German ballet* with a high standard was established by calling on the services of choreographers such as George Balanchine, Tatjana Gsovsky, John Cranko and Kenneth MacMillan, by setting-up ballet schools and continually engaging top-rank performers and ensembles from other lands.

The film industry enjoys the limelight at the annual cultural and documentary film weeks in Mannheim and Oberhausen, at festivals in Munich and Berlin where young film and television producers such as *489 Alexander Kluge, 487 Peter Lilienthal* and *488 Peter Zadek* compete at international level with their latest films.

*512* Modern art offered by gallery artists such as *Jule Hammer*, painters
*491* and sculptors such as *Horst Antes, 490 E. W. Nay* and *507 Hans Uhl-*
*333* *mann* is displayed at ,,*documenta*" in Kassel, an international exhibition held every four years, and at the Cologne Art Market.

Not without some justification is the world-wide idea of Germany linked with the image of an industrial nation which strove for industrial stabilization following the total collapse in 1945. The cliché of the work-mad German seemed to be confirmed. But not hard work alone made the economic miracle possible. The generous economic aid with its prime-ignition effect which was received within the framework of
*324* the *Marshall Plan* and which began on the initiative of the US President Truman and G. C. Marshall plus the international complexity of German industry were also major contributory factors, as well as the establishment of the economic policy of free marketing under Konrad Adenauer and Ludwig Erhard. The realisation that a single state could not create highly-developed technology in all branches of the econ-
*453–456* omy and the readiness for an international *distribution of work* produced the situation where the Federal Republic of Germany was able to consolidate its efforts and regain world reputation, particularly
*413* in the fields of *synthetics* and *mineral oil processing*, in *339, 400 chemical products, 411, 414, 416 machinery, vehicle and ship-building* and *electrotechnics.*

Cooperation in the European Organization for Nuclear Physics Re-
*398* search (CERN), the *European Organization for Space Research* (ESRO) and other international scientific organizations, the continual inter-
*312* national *meetings of Nobel prizewinners* in Lindau on Lake Constance revived old German traditions in this field likewise.
*334* Scientists such as *Feodor Lynen*, who received the Nobel Prize for
*312* Medicine in 1904, the Nobel Prize Winner for Physics in 1961 *Rudolf*
*316* *Mössbauer* and the Nobel Prize Winner *Werner Heisenberg* integrate the German contribution in a world-wide context.

Although it can hardly be expected that the rapid rise in the gross national product in the last 20 years – over 500 $^0/_0$ since 1950 – will continue at the same pace in the future, economics experts forecast a considerable growth in the gross national product in the Federal Republic with increasing export possibilities and a progressive economic policy aimed at stability and expansion. This expansion offers the continuing prerequisites for social security.

This very stress on export by the German economy implies a particular
*421-426 commitment.* Technological progress and a high standard of living cannot remain the prerogative of the industrial nations in a world of poverty and distress. Growing populations and the serious economic problems of the under-developed parts of the world make the energetic help of all industrial powers essential. The Federal Republic, as one of the richest countries on earth, with an expenditure on aid of over DM 40,000 millions since 1950, is, on a per-capita basis, one of the leaders in fostering progress in developing lands.

What is Germany today? A nation of two states, fourth largest industrial power in the world, partner of the developing countries, example of a society in the process of democratisation, cross-roads of artistic tradition and artistic progress, focal point of European integration and a staunch member of the Atlantic Community.